New Horse Handbook

The Wild Horse: An Adopter's Manual,
co-authored with Barbara Eustis-Cross

John Rarey: Horse Tamer

New Horse Handbook
Settling in Safely at a New Stable

Nancy Bowker

STERLING PUBLISHING CO., INC.
NEW YORK

Disclaimer

This book contains the opinions and ideas of its author. It is intended to provide helpful and informative material on the subject covered. It is sold with the understanding that the author and publisher are not engaged in rendering professional services in the book. The reader should consult a competent professional for personal assistance or advice.

The author and publisher specifically disclaim any responsibility for any liability, loss, or risk, personal or otherwise, which is incurred as a consequence, directly or indirectly, of the use and application of any of the contents of this book.

Library of Congress Cataloging-in-Publication Data avaiable

Unless otherwise noted, all photographs by Karin Naimark.

10 9 8 7 6 5 4 3 2 1

Published by Sterling Publishing Co., Inc.
387 Park Avenue South, New York, NY 10016
© 2003 by Nancy Bowker
Distributed in Canada by Sterling Publishing
^{c}/o Canadian Manda Group, One Atlantic Avenue, Suite 105
Toronto, Ontario, Canada M6K 3E7
Distributed in Great Britain by Chrysalis Books
64 Brewery Road, London N7 9NT, England
Distributed in Australia by Capricorn Link (Australia) Pty. Ltd.
P.O. Box 704, Windsor, NSW 2756, Australia

Printed in China
All rights reserved

Sterling ISBN 0–8069–8815–0

To Jess

an extraordinary daughter and friend,

whose passion embraces

the entire animal kingdom.

Contents

Preface

For people who love horses, there is a special time when excitement runs as high as a little foal on a fair and breezy day. This special period occurs as you anticipate the arrival of a new horse in your barn or as you prepare to move your horse to a new stable.

You need to make many decisions during these busy days. As an owner, you want to ensure that your horse will be comfortable, and you want to avoid situations in which your horse could be hurt. This book is designed to help make this important transition time safer and easier for you and your horse.

Note that throughout the book, the masculine gender is used to refer to horses, except when specifically referring to fillies and mares.

Acknowledgments

I extend my deepest appreciation to the following friends, family members, and professionals for their invaluable help, expertise, and assistance:

My daughter, Jessica Bowker, for working with me through the midnight hour and listening to endless horse stories; my editor, Madelyn Larsen, whose precise editing and consideration for horses brought this book to completion; the inspiring life and work of the great horse trainer John S. Rarey and his stallion Cruiser.

My equine experts and friends: Robin Rivello and Reno; Lyn Kamer; Loretto McCartney; Thomas W. Brooks; Mary Regler; Judy Lewis; Brenda Ciribassi; Gail Morton; Mary Lee Shalayda; Karen Froberg, DVM; Julia Allerton, DVM; Daniel Keenan, DVM; Barbara Shuster, DVM; farrier Mark VandeGrift; equine dental technician Scott Gager; Elsie Rarey; Maxine Drury; historian Richard Palsgrove, Director of the Groveport Heritage Museum in Ohio for his excellent work in preserving the history of the town where Rarey and Cruiser lived; Anita Curtis, Jean Grim, and Penelope Smith, whose compassionate work is bringing the inner world of animals into public awareness.

My personal support team: Carol Vento; Russ Bowker; Melinda Wardwell; James and Timothy Souder; Dennis Wilno; and the staff of the Burlington County Library in Westampton,

New Jersey for checking out all those books; the staff at Sterling Publishers; my friends and co-workers at Barnes & Noble Book-sellers in Moorestown, New Jersey, especially Annette Miller, Gretchen Rector, Lori Paulino, and Mary Jo Sell; my writer's group: Beverly Haaf, Anna Hageman, Dina Leacock, and Marie Wise, who cheerfully endured a year of horse chapters.

To my wise and witty horses, Sierra and Battle Clip, and to the memory of my mares, Idget and Bonfire, for teaching a hard-headed little person to listen on the inside; and to Saint George, patron saint of horses, may his protection spread far and wide.

I am also indebted to photographer Karin Naimark for her beautiful images, generous patience, and friendship during all our hours together; and to her daughter, Jessica Naimark, for being a wonderful and gracious model, along with her handsome horse, Charlie.

Karin Naimark, in turn, would like to thank: Ryan M. Allison; Momi K. Black; Stephen Bokman, DVM; Nancy, Russ and Jessica Bowker; Anne Byrne; Christine M. Calandra; Lynn Colombaris; Hans Dressler; Norma C. House; Hugo Huesca; Lyn Kamer; Doug King; David J. Laurick; Dana LoGalbo; James Maillet; Jessica Naimark; Bryant Pace; Charles T. Palmer III; Ashley Partow; Andrew H. Philbrick; Susannah Wise Philbrick; Robin Rivello; Sarah Rockoff; Mary Lee Shalayda; Linda Sheridan; Kim W. Sloan; James S. Souder; Gail F. Strecker; Linda Toscano; Caroline Vander Hyden; and Melinda Wardwell.

In addition, I want to thank the following farms for their help: Boxwood Farm, Hunter Farms, Irene's Spring Tree Farm, and Wildflowers Farm.

Finally, my heartfelt thanks and gratitude to my loving family: Richard, Jessica, and Sam Naimark, and to my parents, Martin and Lilo, for all their help and support.

Introduction

The idea for this book came from the distant memory of a chestnut mare, a time of an extraordinary thrill. When I was fourteen, after years of cleaning stalls in exchange for riding and endless hours spent poring over horse books, my sister, Melinda, and I finally talked Mom and Dad into getting a horse. Sweet promises of endless housework and continual goodness turned the tide. Following this victory came the search, discovery, and purchase of a Quarter Horse mare. She was named Bonfire, or Bonnie, for her flaming red coat.

On a cold morning in January, Bonnie was en route to her new home. We had rented a stall at a nearby farm, and we were waiting there for her to arrive. The hour when she was due came and went. I remember tramping out her name in the snow to fill the anxious minutes. After another hour ticked by, my hopes were falling as fast as the icicles plummeting from the barn roof.

Finally, Melinda shouted, "There she is!"

Spinning around with a rush of joy, I saw the welcome sight of the truck and trailer rumbling up the lane. The driver parked near the pasture. He opened the back ramp of the trailer, and there she was. When he unhooked the tail bar, Bonnie scrambled backwards out of the trailer.

"Whoa!" he yelled.

She stopped, swinging her head to the side as if expecting a blow. Standing like a statue, she turned and focused her eyes on the horses cantering up from the pasture to see this new horse. I was in awe of her. I absolutely loved the fire gleaming in her eyes, the crooked white stripe on her face that looked as if it had been painted on by an artist with a shaky hand, and her long red mane and tail rippling in the icy wind.

Her nostrils flared, and she blasted a "Honk," the danger snort. She followed that with an ear-splitting whinny that shook her whole body from ears to tail.

"What's the matter with her?" Melinda yelled.

"She's just a little scared," the driver replied. "New places, new horses, and she's looking for her friends."

His words hit me like a thunderbolt. Until that moment, I had never realized it would be as frightening for her coming here as it was for me on the first day of school every year.

Handing Melinda the lead rope, he said, "She's all yours," and breathed out a huff of relief. Lifting up the trailer ramp, he added, "Goodbye and good luck."

As he pulled away, Bonnie gave one last sorrowful whinny as if to say, "Why are you leaving me here with these strangers?"

One of the horses in the field whinnied back. Bonnie's eyes widened in fear. Ready or not, her new life had begun.

By the end of that first day, we had made a lot of mistakes that we didn't even know were mistakes at the time. We fed Bonnie our local grain and hay without gradually changing to it from her usual food. We had never even asked what kind she was getting. Fortunately, she didn't develop colic or come down with laminitis.

Our next big blunder on the first day was turning her out in the pasture with the other horses. First of all, had she been sick, she would have given her infection to the other horses. Second, the encounter was a disaster. We watched in horror as the hooves flew, teeth snapped, and our darling mare was chased, kicked, and bitten. It was a nasty reception for her. Luckily, she wasn't seriously injured, but she did sport some missing tufts of hair on her flanks and hindquarters.

Another bad idea was riding her that day, as if she hadn't had enough traumas.

While grooming her, I soon discovered some unpleasant surprises. She did not like her back hooves handled and would gladly kick you if you tried. We had never handled her feet, nor did we saddle her ourselves. She wasn't fond of being tacked up either and attempted to take out a couple of my ribs as I was pulling up the girth.

Undaunted, out into the riding ring we went. Melinda, being older and stronger, rode her first. They got along fine. Then I got on. I found out that she didn't like to stop, even when heading straight towards a fence. I instantly learned why some horses are called hard-mouthed. She preferred to smash into the gate like a crash-test dummy rather than listen to a rein urging a turn.

We quickly came to the sad conclusion that Bonnie must have been drugged when we went to see her. We had only visited her once and that was announced well in advance.

We kept her though, until the day that summer when a canter on the trails turned into a runaway gallop. In the movies, it never looks scary when the cowboys are zooming along. But in real life, it felt like a headlong rush to disaster. We made it back in record time. She slid to a stop in front of the barn door and literally threw me inside.

After that episode, Mom insisted that she wanted us to have more birthdays, and we would have to part ways with iron-jaw Bonnie. We sold her to a man who was well aware of her problems and said he could work with her. I hope he was a gentleman.

Despite all the troubles, it was a sad day when he came to get her. It was terrible seeing her being loaded in the trailer and hearing her frightened whinnies all the way down the lane. After this, Melinda and I both got jobs and bought our own horses, Patsy and Idget. We had a lot of fun and frustration with them both.

Looking back now, many years and horses later (my own and those I cared for at breeding, show, and racing stables), I realize that a lot of the problems may have resulted from having such a rocky start. It may have set off a strong resistance and distrust in Bonnie that could never be erased. If she had been given recovery time to settle in and get over all the bewildering changes before expecting her to do anything, things might have gone smoother with our chestnut bombardier.

This book is an attempt to help all the scared, lonely horses moving into new stables as well as those who care for them and about them. May we all relate to our horses in the quiet way that says, "Relax, you are safe with me."

New Horse Handbook

1 Before the Van Arrives

Before the van arrives, you'll have days of anticipation, fun, and planning. Welcoming a new horse or preparing your current horse to relocate involves arranging housing and transport. It also requires giving some thought to the horse's heightened emotional needs during the transition.

We'll explore his emotional needs first. What are a horse's feelings when he is separated from the herd and moved to a strange location? He will probably be frightened and insecure because he will be without the three things that a horse usually relies on for a sense of well-being.

THE HERD. The strongest equine instinct is to live in a herd, so naturally a horse feels safe in the presence of other horses. He also feels comfortable with having a well-defined place in the herd's social order and a friend to groom with and to graze beside.

HOME BASE. A horse develops strong attachments to his stall, barn, and pasture and to personal items such as halters and feed and water buckets.

FAMILIAR FACES AND ROUTINES. A horse prefers his days to follow a routine. He wants to see the same people doing their regular jobs at the same time each day, and he wants a special person who bestows a daily dose of comforting affection.

The herd is a horse's security blanket.

The horse that is sold and moved to a new location suddenly loses all of his security. As a result, the horse will be on edge and emotionally vulnerable during the transitional days. Therefore, the focus should be on maintaining a soothing and reassuring manner with him. Chapter 2 will detail some ways to help your horse feel more at ease in his new home.

Housing

During their thousands of years of interaction with mankind, horses have lived in varied landscapes. They have left their half-circle hoofprints all over the globe, from the sweeping open steppes of Mongolia to the rocky coasts of the British Isles and

All horses enjoy the attention and affection of a special person.

from the swirling desert sands of the Sahara back to their place of origin in North America.

Obviously, horses can adapt to the different housing situations provided for them such as corrals, stables, fields, barns and even tents, yurts, and royal palaces. However, they will settle in with

the most confidence if their new arrangement is similar to their old living situation.

For example, if the horse you are buying or moving is pasture-kept now, he is accustomed to the freedom to move about. Suddenly confining him to a stall would be very stressful for him. On the other hand, a horse accustomed to a stall would be equally upset by staying outdoors around the clock.

The shock of abrupt changes in environment can cause physical and mental stress and disorders. Gradual changes are always the best policy when dealing with a horse's housing, feeding, and grazing in new pastures.

Before your horse comes home, here are some other things to be aware of and to take care of while preparing for his arrival.

QUARANTINE. Most boarding stables automatically quarantine a new horse to prevent the spread of disease. They keep a new horse in a separate field, barn, or in another part of the main barn. In addition to separating a new horse, the staff takes special

Pasture-kept horses will appreciate the same environment in their new home.

Far left: An example of a well-maintained and attractive stable.

precautions, such as washing their hands and changing their clothes and boots, after caring for a new horse. They know how important it is to be careful about transmitting diseases, especially in show and sale stables where horses are continually coming and going. Although a horse may not appear to be ill, he could be a carrier.

One morning at the farm where my sister, Melinda, and I boarded our horses, Idget and Patsy, a new mare moved in. A week later, the stable where the mare came from reported several deaths from equine infectious anemia, or E.I.A. The new mare showed no sign of illness, but the owner had her tested.

The tests showed the mare was a carrier of E.I.A., and, tragically, she had to be put down. In the meantime, our horses were tested, too. While waiting for the results, the horses had to stay in the barn day and night in the middle of a hot spell. This prevented them from being bitten by mosquitoes and spreading the disease. After a worrisome week, the results came back; fortunately, our horses were fine. The crisis was over for us, but we felt sorry for the mare and her owner.

If you are importing a horse from another country, you must follow specific governmental regulations. Any horse being imported into the United States arrives at one of these ports of entry: Newburgh, New York; Newark, New Jersey; Los Angeles, California; Miami, Florida; or Honolulu, Hawaii. All horses undergo a 72-hour quarantine at the port of entry. According to United States Department of Agriculture (U.S.D.A.) regulations, fillies and colts two years old and under and geldings of any age that test free of disease are released. Any horse that appears sick or feverish must remain in quarantine.

Stallions and mares over the age of two are quarantined at the port of entry and then taken to a U.S.D.A. quarantine station for an additional quarantine period. These stations are located in eighteen states at U.S.D.A.-approved farms and universities. The owner may choose the facility. Testing is carried out there for contagious equine metritis (C.E.M). This is a serious bacterial infection seen in mares. Experts believe it is spread by stallions who act as carriers. This additional quarantine process takes

approximately four to five weeks. During this period, the horse will also be wormed and vaccinated for U.S. diseases.

PROTECTION. Separating your horse from the others is also beneficial for his own protection. A horse's instinct is to reject and drive away any new horse in the pasture. The equine view is that someone is invading his territory, and strangers bring dangers. So, besides the need for quarantine, your horse will be safer in his own stall or paddock where he can't be harassed. The ideal arrangement is for him to be apart but still be able to see and hear other horses.

DIET. What you will feed your horse when he first moves in is crucial; his life could depend on the right diet. An abrupt switch in his diet could bring on a case of colic or laminitis. Details on these problems will be discussed later in the chapter. A gradual changeover to new hay and grain is the key, mixing in the new with the old, little by little. Therefore, before your horse arrives, you'll need to buy some of the same type of hay and grain that he is eating now.

A LOCAL VET AND FARRIER. Establishing a connection with a vet and farrier prior to your horse's arrival ensures that if anything happens while traveling to your new stable or immediately afterward, you'll have someone to call. You will need their services soon anyway for routine visits and care.

REFERENCE BOOKS. Purchase at least one book on veterinary care to have on hand for the everyday problems that crop up such as mysterious bumps and minor cuts. You will also want to consult a book to help identify the symptoms that require a call to the vet.

NECESSARY PAPERWORK. Before your horse can travel, you will need a Coggins test for E.I.A, a health certificate from the veterinarian that is no more than thirty days old, and possibly a brand inspection from the state brand inspector. The states that require a brand inspection are Arizona, Colorado, Idaho, Montana, Nevada, New Mexico, Utah, and Wyoming. Certain parts of Nebraska, Oregon, and Washington require it as well.

PLANS FOR EMERGENCIES. If you do not own a trailer, locate someone who could transport your horse to an emergency veterinary clinic if the need arises. Put maps to the clinic and phone numbers in a place you'll remember. Also, find a nearby stable where you could bring your horse if something should happen to your farm. Sudden events can occur that might damage your barn or knock down your pasture fence.

TRAVELING EQUIPMENT. Plan to have the following items on hand when you transport your horse.

Before putting shipping boots or bandages on, check the hooves for stones or any debris that could cause discomfort during travel. When wrapping the legs, make sure you cover the coronary band and fasten the ties on the outside of the leg.

- Shipping boots or bandages and leg wraps. If your horse is being shipped a long distance (eight to twelve hours or more on a commercial van), leave the boots off. They could impair circulation in the legs by being on that long, and the handlers will not remove them.
- Poll guard to protect his head.
- Blanket. If the weather is very cold or if the horse is chilled, you will need a blanket. In most seasons though, horses are generally safer without one. A blanket could get caught on something and cause the horse to panic. The horse could also become overheated as a result of nervous sweating or a lack of fresh air inside the trailer.

- Extra halter and lead rope. The primary traveling halter should be leather, not rope or nylon, to allow for the halter to break or be cut off in an emergency.

FIRST-AID KIT. Assemble a kit to keep at the barn; bring it along if you will be transporting the horse. The kit should include the following:

- Rolls of sheet cotton, stretch gauze, adhesive wrap bandages, and tape.
- Cold packs for injuries. Before applying to the skin, place a piece of cotton or a towel between the pack and the skin to avoid frostbite.
- Ointment. A first-aid antibiotic cream with pain relief medication is a good choice.
- Antiseptic wash, such as a peroxide or iodine solution.
- Coagulant powder to stop bleeding.
- Clean towels, washcloths, sponges, and a bucket.
- Scissors, duct tape, and a camping knife.
- Equine thermometer with a long string attached or an electronic digital thermometer.
- Eyewash, drawing salve, poultice, Epsom salts, and mineral oil.
- Spray bottle with sterile saline solution to clean wounds.
- Stethoscope to determine heart rate and respiration and to check gut sounds.

TIME. Schedule a generous block of time for the day of the move, even if it's a short trip in miles. If you can, arrange to leave in the morning when you have the whole day ahead of you. This will allow the horse to settle in before night. Arriving at dusk increases the horse's suspicions about his new surroundings.

A horse's eye structure permits him to see well in low light. However, his eyes, like those of dogs and cats, adjust more slowly to darkness than ours do. As a result, when a horse is first shown a dimly lit barn or trailer, it looks like a gloomy cave with no escape route.

Transport

For a horse, any travel is stressful, whether the distance is short or long. The horse is leaving home and going to an unknown destination.

Studies have shown that any horse, no matter what age, gender, or experience with shipping, gets upset when confronted

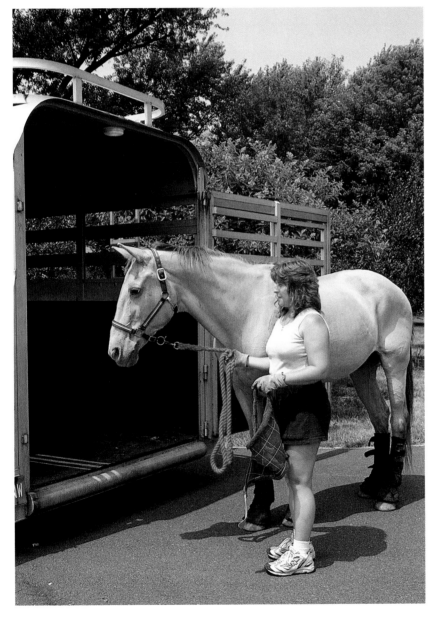

Loading is a nervous time for a horse even if he appears unruffled. Wearing gloves while loading a horse is a good idea.

with a trailer. The physical indicators of stress, heart rate and cortisol levels in the blood, all shoot up whether the horse appears to be anxious or calm. This is also a time of danger because most injuries occur during loading and unloading.

Do not give tranquilizers before transport unless absolutely necessary. It may seem like a good idea to calm the horse down, but it can backfire. Tranquilized horses can become unstable and fall, and the drugs can cause a dangerous rise in the horse's temperature.

A fly mask protects the horse's eyes from particles and dust while en route.

Considerations for traveling

LENGTH OF TRIP. Research reveals that the longer the horse is on the road, the greater his chance of becoming ill. A dramatic increase in physical disorders occurs after twelve hours of transport; another large increase in cases of illness occurs after twenty hours of continuous travel.

Ideally, you should stop the trailer at least every two hours to check on the horse, offer water, and let him rest for a few moments. The constant effort to balance himself while the trailer is moving is very tiring. Experts estimate that for every hour the horse is hauled, the physical effort involved is the same as if he had walked that far; so three hours of transport equals three hours of walking.

After being on the road for four hours, you should take the horse off the trailer if a safe location is available. Allow him to drink, stretch his legs, and urinate. Horses usually urinate every

Offer water at every rest stop. On average, horses drink twelve gallons a day. When working hard or in hot weather, that amount may double and even triple, especially during periods of extreme heat and humidity. Photo by the author.

two to four hours, and some will not feel comfortable about urinating in a trailer.

JIGGLE OF THE JOURNEY. The movement of the trailer affects the horse's internal organs as well. A horse's hooves vibrate at the same rate as the trailer, but his internal organs vibrate at a higher level. This leads to body stress and exhaustion. Take this into consideration and drive at lower speeds whenever possible. Accelerate gradually, use wide turns, and brake carefully.

HEAD POSITION. In the trailer, tying the horse's head up high with his ears above the withers can start a harmful chain of events. Tie his head so that the horse has some range of motion. However, the rope should not be so long that he could get a leg over it. Horses clear their throats by putting their noses down; this removes dust and bacteria. When the head is forced to remain up, bacteria can move down into the lungs and cause infections.

PLACEMENT ON THE TRAILER. If you are hauling one horse, put him on the left side. This provides better balance. If you are moving two horses, put the heftier one on the left.

FOOD AND WATER DURING TRANSIT. Here are some things to keep in mind:

■ Hay. Let the horse have plenty of the hay he is used to eating. Chewing on hay helps to keep him occupied; it also assists in keeping water in his intestines. This is important to avoid colic. Select hay with the least amount of loose particles. You don't want him to inhale flying hay bits during the trip because this could result in choking or coughing.
■ Water. Dehydration is dangerous and can occur during longer trips. Offer a drink every two hours or every hour in very hot weather. Use water from the horse's former home if possible. Frequently, horses won't trust the scent of strange water or strange buckets and will refuse to drink.
■ Grain. Hold back on giving any grain for several hours before

your horse goes on the trailer. Do not give any grain at all during the trip. Your horse will be fine with just hay. The upset of travel can slow or stop the working of the horse's intestines. If this happens, any grain he has eaten could start to ferment, causing colic or even laminitis.

All of the above factors combine to challenge the body's defenses. The immune system continues to be weak for twenty-four hours or longer after transport, depending on the distance traveled. As a rule, for every twelve hours of transport, the horse needs one complete day of rest.

When the immune system is compromised by travel stress, the horse is at risk for several major problems. The following illnesses frequently occur to horses not carefully transported. These illnesses are described briefly to make you aware of symptoms that could possibly affect your horse's life.

Hay helps to keep your horse content during transport.

Colic

This painful condition is caused by gas in the intestines or obstructions resulting from the ingestion of sand, parasites, food, or even foreign materials such as plastic. For the horse, it must feel like having a storm raging inside. Always take colic seriously; it can be fatal.

Symptoms

The horse

- Acts restless and agitated, walks in circles, and sweats.
- Keeps looking back; may nip or kick at his flanks.
- Repeatedly lies down to roll and then gets back up.
- Swishes his tail, paws the ground, and yawns frequently.
- Stamps his hind hooves or switches weight from one hind hoof to the other.
- Produces only a small amount of manure or urine or none at all.
- Produces gut sounds that reverberate with extra noisy gurgling or the "ping" noises indicating a gas buildup.
- Does not produce any gut sounds, indicating digestion has stopped. (This is very serious and could indicate an impaction, a blockage of material in the intestines.)

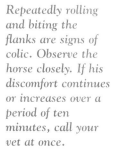

Repeatedly rolling and biting the flanks are signs of colic. Observe the horse closely. If his discomfort continues or increases over a period of ten minutes, call your vet at once.

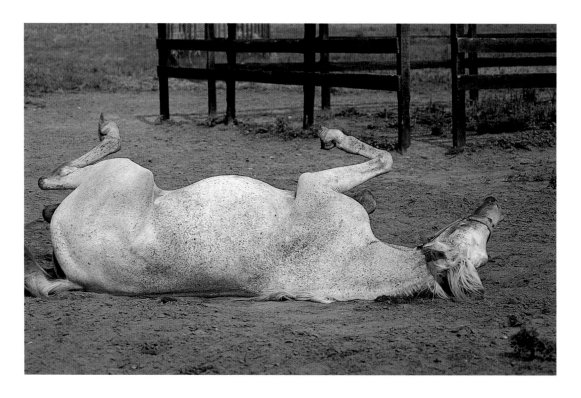

- Thrashes violently from the intense discomfort of the later stages of colic. (Because you cannot do much to stop the horse, stay out of the way. Always be careful around any horse that is colicky. No matter how even-tempered ordinarily, any horse in pain can become dangerous and bite or lash out with a hoof.)

If the horse is not in too much distress, take his vital signs so you can report them to the vet when you call. This will give the vet an idea how serious the colic is and what stage it's in.

Vital signs

HEART RATE. A normal adult horse's pulse rate is thirty to forty-four beats a minute. Very young horses register faster beats, but older horses have a slower rate. A good place to find the pulse is by the jawbone at the maxillary artery. Count for fifteen seconds and multiply by four to get the rate.

RESPIRATION. One inhalation and exhalation equals one breath; ten to fifteen breaths a minute is normal. Hot weather produces more rapid breathing; foals breathe faster than adults.

RATIO OF HEART RATE TO RESPIRATION. Normally, this ranges between 4 to 1 and 2 to 1. A change of 1 to 1 or 1 to 2 is a serious symptom. Report this to the vet immediately.

TEMPERATURE. The average is between 99 and 101.5 degrees F. Anything over 103 degrees at rest is a concern; 105 degrees or higher is serious. Temperatures below normal, in the 97.5 to 99 degree range, could indicate shock; 97 degrees or below is a symptom of a life-threatening problem.

GUMS. A pale pink color is normal; white gums could signal shock or anemia. The gums are a rich pink if the horse was just exercising. Bright red is very alarming and could indicate poisoning. Gums having a deep brick-red or purple appearance indicate a serious illness.

While waiting for the vet

- Take away any grain or hay in the stall. Water can remain.
- If the horse does drop manure, leave it. It can give the vet clues about what is going on internally.
- In a mild case of colic, walking the horse and letting him graze may help to liberate gas. Gently massaging his ears may make the horse more comfortable because acupressure points in the ears are linked to nerves in the abdomen and intestines.
- Don't force a horse up if he is determined to lie down. Vets advise letting him do so. It's better for the horse to stay calm rather than undergo the upset of being forced up.
- Do not give any painkilling medication. The vet needs to see his exact condition.

When the vet arrives

The vet will begin a careful examination of the horse by asking about his symptoms and by taking his vital signs. Treatment depends on the extent and type of colic. The vet will often give an antispasmodic or a painkilling drug first; then, he will use a stomach tube to administer warm water, mineral oil, or a laxative to get the blockage moving. More serious cases, such as a twisted intestine or a solid impaction, may require surgery.

At a farm where I once worked, I saw a colic case involving a mare with a filly alongside. A few days after they were shipped in, the mare showed signs of severe colic. The vet came and tried everything possible. However, a day later, the mare went into endotoxemia, or blood poisoning, and the decision was made to put her down. The filly kept whinnying for her. Hearing her desperate calling was heart-rending.

Colic is the number one killer of domestic horses, so it is imperative that you secure a professional evaluation if you suspect colic.

Laminitis

Laminitis, also known as founder in the chronic stage, is another very serious condition. In this case, the flow of blood in and out of the hoof, called the vascular balance, is upset. This causes too much blood to pool in the feet. In other words, too much blood is going down into the hooves and not enough is going back up the leg.

The congestion causes the sensitive tissue inside the hoof, the laminae, to become inflamed and to swell. The hooves cannot expand, and so they hurt. In human terms, this is like having size 9 feet but wearing size 7 boots.

An attack can be triggered by:

■ Confinement for long periods of time. When the horse has no exercise and too much feed during long-distance road travel, air transport, or a sea voyage, the lack of exercise can lead to laminitis.

Cooling a horse thoroughly after exercise is very important in preventing laminitis. Photo by the author.

- A sudden influx of feed. For example, when a horse breaks into a feed bin and overeats, laminitis can result.
- Rich, green grass. If you let a horse graze too long on new spring grass or a new growth of fall grass after a summer drought, the grass will overtax his system, setting the stage for laminitis. Moving the horse from a poor pasture to an area with lush grass can have the same effect.
- Excessive work when the horse is not fit. When the horse is not cooled out properly after exercise, allowed to drink large quantities of water, and left to stand when hot, the vascular balance in the hooves is upset.
- Lameness in one front leg. When a horse is lame in a front leg, more weight will be placed on the other leg. If this continues for a long time, laminitis may develop in the formerly sound leg.

Symptoms

- Walking slowly and painfully, as if on red-hot sand. The horse is reluctant to put any weight on the tender hoof. Trouble commonly occurs in one or both front hooves. While standing or walking, the horse may shift his weight to the hind legs.
- A rise in temperature and sweating.
- Increased digital pulse. A pounding pulse can be felt behind the pastern. Normally, it's hard to detect the pulse here, so if it's noticeable, it is a symptom of inflammation.
- Warm hoof. This is another sign of inflammation.
- Lack of interest in food. He refuses feed or nibbles only a little.

While waiting for the vet

- Leave the horse in a stall or paddock.
- Do not give any grain, but you may give a small amount of low-protein hay.
- Weather permitting, cool the hooves with running water from a hose for no more than five minutes every thirty minutes. The time between allows the blood to circulate.

At all costs, avoid laminitis. The horse experiences terrible pain, and laminitis may be followed by long-term problems. Many horses are unsound for months afterwards, and some are lame forever. Unfortunately, the most severely affected horses suffer so much that they are humanely destroyed, like the great racehorse Secretariat.

After the attack, it can take a year for the hoof to look normal again. It can appear distorted with characteristic ridges and a dished look. The hoof wall is weakened and apt to crack. It may also develop an abscess.

When an abscess does occur, sand or gravel has gotten up inside the hoof wall, inflaming it and causing the horse to become lame. An opening has to be made for the infected material to drain out. In order to do this, the vet or farrier makes an opening; then, the hoof needs to be soaked daily, packed with drawing salve, and bandaged.

My mare Sierra once had laminitis. Her mustang courage kept her going day by day, even when it must have been awful to get up and move around. Eventually, she was able to walk without pain, but that did not happen for a long time. She's a trooper, and I admire her courage and will power. When she's cantering around the field, mane and tail flying, it's a sight I certainly do not take for granted.

Shipping fever

Shipping fever is a highly contagious condition, a form of pleuro-pneumonia, in which symptoms can rapidly appear. Fluid fills the cavity around the lungs and can become infected. The horse can be out of work for weeks. In more serious cases, he can be disabled for life or even die.

Research findings point to strep bacteria that live in the upper respiratory system as the cause. In healthy horses, the throat and airways have a coating that catches germs and dust. They also have a protein in the coating that fights infection.

When the airways dry out from dust and not drinking enough, the amount of protein is reduced, so bacteria can get through easier and go down into the lungs. If the horse's head is kept tied in a high position, this doubles the opportunity for the bacteria to invade the lungs.

Symptoms

- Listless behavior. The horse appears depressed. The head frequently droops, and the throat glands may swell.
- Runny nose and eyes. Bright light bothers the eyes.
- Pink eye. The white around the eye, the conjunctiva, can become red.
- Fever. A temperature of 103 to 106 degrees F. is common. The fever can last for three days.
- Not eating or eating very little.
- Shallow and rapid breathing.

- Isolate the horse and wash your hands and change your clothes before interacting with other horses.
- Keep the horse warm with blankets if the weather is cold. In hot weather, protect him from flies.
- Provide absolute rest with access to fresh air and plenty of drinking water.
- Allow a small amount of hay and reduce the grain ration.

Vets will often prescribe a course of antibiotics. During the recovery period, the horse has to rest for a few weeks to prevent a relapse. Discuss with your vet a program for the horse's gradual return to work.

Tying-up

Tying-up is a muscle disorder involving painful spasms and cramps, especially in the back and hindquarters. When traveling long distances, the muscles can become inflamed from standing in one spot too long. Dehydration is also suspected as a cause.

This condition is sometimes referred to as azoturia, or Monday morning disease, because it was common among workhorses resuming work on Monday after the weekend off. A combination of full grain ration and no exercise was thought to cause the problem. Standard advice is to cut the horse's grain in half when he's not working.

Symptoms

- Walking stiffly. This is most noticeable in the hind legs. When the muscles start to spasm, the horse will breathe hard, sweat, and have a worried expression.
- Elevated pulse rate.
- Change in color of the urine. In severe cases, urine can appear red or as dark as black tea. The color change is caused by the

myoglobin in the affected muscles going into the blood. Report this to your vet.

The combination of standing still for extended hours in the trailer and dehydration can lead to the muscle disorder tying-up. Rest horses every four hours on long journeys.

While waiting for the vet

- If the horse is at an event, stop riding immediately. Any further exercise can do more damage. Keep the horse warm and take him home.
- Lightly massage the muscles to help alleviate the pain. If the contact is too irritating to the horse, just let him rest.

During the vet's examination, he or she may take a blood sample. This will show the seriousness of the attack and determine how soon the horse can slowly return to work. During recovery, the horse's food and the amount of it are important, so consult your veterinarian. Many vets will recommend a bran mash or laxative diet.

This is a lot of medical information to absorb, but it's better to be informed about health matters for your horse's sake. Remember, the day is drawing near when all the planning, packing, and preparation will be finished, and you and your horse will be on your way to a new adventure.

2 Moving into a New Home

When the trailer bearing your horse finally rumbles up the lane, it's both a relief and a thrill. For your horse, a challenging time of excitement and uncertainty lies ahead. Once he comes off the trailer, you may be surprised at his behavior. Horses will react differently to being in new surroundings, depending on several variables.

TEMPERAMENT AND BREED TYPE. High-strung and hot-blooded horses like Thoroughbreds and Arabians may be nervous and

Home at last!

upset for the first few days. Due to their sensitive nature, they generally need longer to trust their new environment and handlers. Of course, personality plays a part in their reaction.

Horses with a generally calm disposition, such as Quarter Horses, Morgans, warmbloods, and draft breeds, usually accept change with fewer outward signs of fear. However, they still require quiet handling and consideration. Undoubtedly, they feel insecure and out of place in new surroundings.

A boiling mixture of emotions: excitement, fear, and curiosity are rolled into the first memorable moments after arrival.

AGE. The older the horse, the more times he has probably been relocated, so he may accept being moved quite well. Young horses are sensitive and impressionable, and they may react with more fear. They need extra patience and care during handling.

For horses of any age though, the first experiences are crucial because they will leave a lasting effect. You want your horse to feel safe and welcomed. He needs to feel that this is a good place to be. You can compare the gentleness required with a kindergarten teacher's approach to children on the first day of school. Think about those eager, scared children clutching their lunch boxes, grimly leaving Mom and Dad, and walking through the front door of the school. Remember this scenario as you envision your horse coming into a strange barn and having to cope with a new stall, a new pasture, new people, and new horses.

PAST EXPERIENCE. What happened to the horse the last time he moved plays a part in what he expects to deal with this time. If it was a negative experience, then the bad memories will prompt

Starting a new life. him to act more threatened and distrustful. Take the getting-to-know-you phase very slowly and allow more physical space between you and the horse until he starts to feel comfortable.

All these variables play their part in motivating your horse's initial behavior. With this in mind, do not condemn your horse for being standoffish or difficult to handle during the first week or two. Reserve your judgment for at least three weeks until he has had a chance to settle in and reveal his true personality.

My two horses had very different backgrounds, and they handled the transition differently. This is how my Standardbred gelding Battle Clip and my Mustang mare Sierra reacted to being moved.

When Clip first arrived at our farm, he walked off the trailer confident as a peacock. He strutted about as if he owned the place and the kingdom beyond. He neighed, and two mares replied to his call. His face lit up with an expression of, " Hello, ladies!" His confidence stemmed from his self-esteem and from his experience and age. He was thirteen years old, and during his long career at the racetrack, he'd been constantly shipped from place to place. He settled in quite quickly.

As to Sierra, we didn't have a farm when we got her, so we brought her to a boarding stable. She was then five years old and wide-eyed with wonder. She was both curious about the other horses in the stable and scared of them. Growing up in a wild band in Nevada, she knew what an unfamiliar horse could expect from the other horses: bites and kicks.

To protect her from the other horses, we put her in a quarantine paddock, but it took days before she started to relax. It was another week after that before she felt confident enough to allow my daughter Jessica and me to come near her without being on guard. Finally, she revealed a good sense of humor, playing tricks and making funny faces to make us laugh.

A year after this, when she moved to our farm, she acted much more self-assured on arrival. But after looking over the pastures, there was something she needed to know. Where were the other horses she knew?

She blasted out a powerful neigh as if to say, "Where is everyone?"

A few seconds later, a faint whinny came rippling through the woods. A horse we didn't even know on another farm about a mile away answered the question of a worried little mare.

"We're over here!"

The goal is for our horses to feel as secure and happy in their new homes as this Mustang mare appears to be.

Arrival day

During this first stimulating day, let your horse rest for a while once he is settled into his new stall or paddock. He will feel disoriented and need some time alone to calm down. Handle him as little as possible; leave grooming for the following day.

If this is a new horse, wait a day or two before inviting friends and family to visit. The horse can then learn to identify you as his primary person. After a few days, you can bring friends over, but only a few at a time.

Later in the day or the next morning, he will probably be

feeling lonely and be glad for some company. This is an opportune time to visit. If this is a horse you've had at another location, he will be very happy to see your familiar face.

A strong bond of friendship with a new horse can grow and develop from spending a lot of quiet hours together in the first few days; in fact, the more time, the better. Sit outside the stall or paddock and just be there so your horse can see you. Let the horse become curious about you. Your manner will convey, "Relax. You are safe with me."

You can foster good feelings by telling the horse how much you appreciate him being here with you. Since most horses appreciate a compliment, it's a good idea to offer words of praise about his appearance.

Speak softly because your horse is highly sensitive to sound. His whole body is designed like a giant motion-and-sound detector to keep a step ahead of predators. Notice how any sudden or unusual sound or movement will cause him to instantly bring up his head, prick his ears, and look in the direction of the noise.

A horse's ears are very mobile. They can rotate like a satellite dish to pick up sound waves from many directions. This is a survival technique, for if a horse can detect a mountain lion's paw crackling a leaf in the bushes behind him, he has a chance to escape before the pounce.

Hooves can also pick up sound vibrations through the ground. They serve as an

Far left: Once rested, most horses will be glad to see a friendly face.

Sierra looks like she's wondering where everybody is.

early warning system for distant stampedes on the prairies or the approach of dangerous storms.

Dietary considerations

As discussed in Chapter 1, what you initially feed your horse is extremely important. A gradual change to new food is the key point; little by little, mix in the new with the old.

GRAIN. The day your horse arrives, omit grain altogether. Let the horse's digestive system rest. Hay is enough. On the second day, give a quarter of the normal grain ration, especially if the horse is in a stall and not getting exercise. After this, if the horse is getting turned out, add a little more grain each day until he is back to a full ration.

When you are changing grain from one type to another, such as from oats to pellets, the standard advice is to add a total of 1/2 a cup of new feed to the regular ration each day, giving 1/4 cup in the morning and 1/4 cup at night. Slowly add a little more each day, subtracting the added amount of new grain from the regular feed. A complete switchover should take three weeks.

Before you feed your horse, always check the bucket to be sure that it is empty. I've found everything from huge spiders and crickets to beetles and baby mice in the buckets in the morning.

HAY. Follow the same regime for hay. Add a small amount of the new hay to each feeding. If you don't have any of the hay your horse was eating in his old home, use grass hay, which will be easier to digest, instead of protein-rich hay like alfalfa. Give a small amount, perhaps half a flake, and check on the horse after an hour or two for any signs of colic.

WATER. Use any remaining water from the horse's old home. Otherwise, just give plenty of fresh water. In hot weather, you could hang two buckets for water. Change them frequently because the water will get dusty and warm.

The second day

For a new horse, the second day is the time to start your regular grooming and handling. Introduce yourself by degrees after the horse appears calm and settled. Talk to him for a few minutes, moving closer every few moments. When you are ready to begin, start with light stroking and contact in areas where the horse can comfortably accept it.

- The area beneath the withers. This is a spot where the mother horse nuzzles a foal to reassure it when frightened. You can approximate this gesture by making a few circles with your fingertips, eventually changing to the flat of your hand.
- Under the neck. Because of the concentration of nerves in this area, stroking under the neck can be very soothing to a horse.
- Shoulders. Horses are usually not ticklish on their shoulders

Introduce yourself by degrees, giving the horse time to get used to you before basic handling begins.

and don't seem to mind being touched there. It's not as threatening as a hand moving towards their face.

- Chest. Horses often enjoy a scratch on the chest in the area where the neck meets the body.
- Top of the neck. Behind the ears on the top of the neck is the "happy boy" or "happy girl" point. When horses are touched there, they will generally perk up their ears, which seems to cheer them up.
- Face. Once your horse accepts your presence, you can try stroking him lightly on the side of the face. A rhythmic stroking on the forehead calms a horse and helps him focus his attention. Many people will do this during vet or farrier appointments. Avoid petting the very end of the nose at first, for it's a sensitive area. Some horses can react with a strike reflex if touched there. This is a survival instinct because predators will grab a horse's muzzle and hold on while the rest of the pack attacks.

Be careful at all times. Be alert to a horse's body language signaling that he is feeling unhappy or threatened. Look for these warning signs: When he flattens his ears back, he indicates, "Go away. I'm getting angry, and I might bite." When he swings his rump towards you, he's saying, "Get out of here." Raising his back hoof off the ground warns, "I will kick if you persist." Snapping his teeth cautions, " I don't want you near me."

Dealing with an aggressive horse

You have to approach an aggressive horse in an authoritative manner to get his respect. Speak in a firm voice and stand your ground. If he snaps at you, show your disapproval by your facial expression and with a harsh word. A horse needs to learn violence won't be tolerated. Sometimes an aggressive horse just needs more space around him to feel safe. Then, he feels he can get away if threatened. Basically, most aggression is rooted in fear or previous abuse. In rare cases, however, horses have been known to be mentally unbalanced.

If your new horse keeps acting like a sour apple after a week, call a veterinarian to discuss the problem and also consult a professional trainer for advice.

Grooming

By the second day, basic grooming can begin. If this is a new horse, take your time with each initial step. Prepare him for the grooming routine by telling him about each thing that you plan to

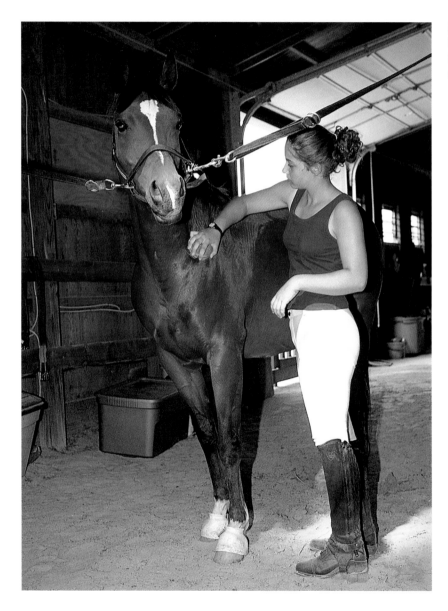

Sensitive grooming helps a horse feel better and improves circulation.

do. For example, say, "I am going to brush you, then comb your mane and tail, and finish by cleaning your hooves." Your quiet reassuring voice will put him at ease.

Remember, when you have finished picking out the hooves, lower the hoof back down slowly. Don't just drop it like a hot potato! Otherwise, you will jar the horse and throw him off balance.

Short sessions of light grooming are best in the beginning. The horse's attention will drift after about ten minutes, so keep the session brief and leave on a pleasant note. It's a victory if your horse looks upon you now as a considerate person who treats him with respect.

The first turnout

If your horse has been in a stall since arrival, by the second day he will be anxious to go out for some exercise. Prior to turnout, inspect the field and fencing. Unless the pasture is the size of Texas, walk along the whole fence line. Look for any weak spots, such as boards down or missing, loose wires, or rusty nails sticking out of boards or on the ground. Remove all trash from the field, including pieces of glass, soda cans, plastic bags, and candy wrappers.

Once you've checked the field, you're ready to walk your horse outside. Expect your horse to be excited at being outdoors again, so safety should be your priority. The first time he goes out sets the pattern in his mind for the manners you will expect of him in the future.

While walking outside, a soft tone of voice directs the horse to focus on you instead of on his anxiety and his desire to break out and run. I find that rather than saying, "It's all right," something like, "What a handsome boy," or "She's such a pretty girl," will draw the horse's attention. It's fun to see the ears perk up at the compliment.

Far left: After being in the stall for the first day, your horse will be glad to go out and explore his new pasture.

Gates and the release

Gates for horses are like intersections for cars; a lot of accidents and injuries happen there. A horse's fear of going through a small opening, coupled with his increasing enthusiasm to be free, spells trouble. Make sure the horse is not crowding you as you approach and go through the gate.

You need to show your horse how you want him to act before you release him. After you walk through the gate, turn around and go back to swing the gate closed. The horse must learn that he needs to wait while you fasten the latch.

Next, walk him around the pasture so he can see the boundaries and the location of the water tub. Return to the gate and stand there for a minute. Talk quietly, stroke him, and take a deep breath. A useful attitude to adopt is, "I have many hours to do this."

At some stables, halters are a necessity in the pasture. But if you can, leave them off.

A small treat, like a tiny piece of carrot, will keep him focused on something good happening while waiting. Many trainers disapprove of giving treats; however, you need to decide for yourself how you feel about them.

When the horse is standing calmly, unclip the lead and let him go. Be prepared though. He might wheel around and take off or even kick. Since I use treats, I give one more treat after I take the halter off to encourage him to wait and not to rush off.

As a rule, it's dangerous to leave halters on horses in the pasture or in the stall. Many terrible accidents have occurred because a halter has snagged on fencing or hooks. In addition, other accidents happen when a hoof catches the halter while the horse is scratching.

Despite the risks, some farms find it absolutely necessary to leave halters on in the field. In this case, a breakaway halter is recommended. That way, if the halter gets caught, the crownpiece breaks and releases the horse.

For the first few times out in a new pasture, leave the halter on until you are positive you can catch your horse. Of course, you'll keep an eye on him while he's in the pasture.

Catching a horse in the pasture

The best scenario is for the horse to come to you. Many horses will hang around the gate when it is time to come in. They're hungry and know food will be served inside the barn.

If your horse is way out in the field grazing, do not approach him from the front or from behind him. Approach him from an angle. Many horses, if approached from behind, will run away. The flank area is a neutral point where the horse is less inclined to go forward or backward.

When you get near him, stop and see if he will come over. Let him become curious. Act as if it's no big deal and you're not in any hurry. If he comes, praise him or give him a treat. This helps ease his fears. Remember that at this point with a new horse, you are still a stranger. The horse doesn't know what to expect and will still be wary of you. Give him confidence that no harm will come if he lets himself be caught.

This is why the whole catching process should be very relaxed. It is also why it's not a good idea to grab his halter and drag him right into the barn. A better way is to wait a couple of minutes

Let the horse discover that you will reward him for coming to you.

and make it a pleasant experience. Show him that coming to you is a wonderful thing.

You won't have to make a big fuss over him every day because horses learn very fast. Once your horse associates being caught with a happy time, he will be much more willing to come. It is extremely important that your horse willingly accept being caught because a horse that's hard to catch is a real nuisance.

The third day

Things calm down by the third day. The horse probably feels somewhat more at ease and like his old self. You could easily give the horse a week to settle in before riding him. However, if you are eager to start riding and he seems fine, the third day should be an acceptable day to start light riding.

Before you saddle up, let the horse outside by himself for a little while. It's better to let him blow off steam before you mount him. You don't want him to feel too frisky and throw you off. Watch him moving freely in the field. Look for any signs of lameness or illness that might have developed from transport or being turned out the day before.

The principle of first impressions with a new horse applies here, too. When getting ready to ride, you are establishing the

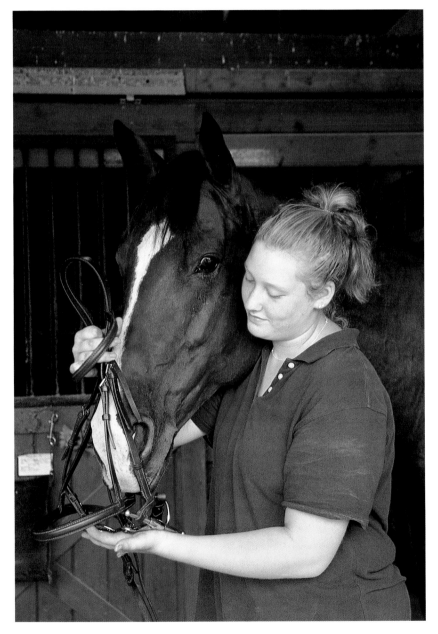

See to your horse's comfort while putting on and adjusting every piece of tack.

rules for how you want him to act during saddling up, mounting, and riding. If he doesn't cooperate right away, remember that your ways of doing things are still strange.

When people become impatient, they become aggressive, and this scares the horse. Communications break down, and the owner and the horse react in self-defense. Therefore, give him extra time

The first time you ride a horse in a new location sets the pattern for future rides, so seek a quiet place.

to understand what you want. Be a calm, cheerful teacher. This will help your horse gain confidence in you. A horse's trust is fragile, but if you are kind and gentle, he will take the chance of trusting you.

3 Keeping Peace in the Pasture

A picture of horses peacefully grazing in a field presents a lovely image. Unfortunately, grazing together often becomes an occasion in which horses ruthlessly chase, bite, and kick each other.

When domestic horses are together, they adhere to the same equine code of conduct their counterparts in the wild do. In other words, they follow a pecking order. It is useful to look at how this social structure works to understand why a new horse entering a herd will be picked on and why he will need protection.

The social order of wild horses

The words "herd" and "band" are important in any discussion of equine groups. A band consists of a stallion, his mares, foals, and one- and two-year-olds; a herd is a larger group of horses that may include several bands. Here is the natural chain of command:

THE STALLION. He is the domineering protector of the band. He places himself at the rear of the group, moving his family away from danger and predators. When another stallion approaches, he'll confront and challenge the intruder. If threats don't work, he'll battle with vicious intensity. An average band has about six

members: the stallion, two or three adult mares, the foals, year-lings, and two-year-olds.

Far left: A new horse is a threat to the existing social structure of the herd.

THE LEAD MARE. She is the leader of the group and chooses the path to the water holes, grazing grounds, and the routes the band uses to escape from enemies. She enforces her dominant position with her teeth and hooves, but usually her threatening gestures are enough to keep the others in line. Her pinned-back ears and the swing of her head say in effect, "I'm the boss; get back." Usually, the other horses will.

OTHER MARES. Each mare has her own place in the chain, depending on how aggressive, old, or compliant she is. The number two mare will pick on the number three mare and so on down the pecking order.

TWO-YEAR-OLD COLTS. Colts at this age are starting to challenge the authority of their sire and dam. By the age of three, sexual tension is rising. At this time, the stallion will drive the colt away, or he will leave on his own.

Solo colts, separated from their parental groups, will join together and form bachelor bands. For a few more years, they will not yet be strong or skillful enough to fight mature stallions and claim mares. In the meantime, they'll test and perfect their warrior skills on each other by nipping and biting, rearing up, and clashing in mock battles.

TWO-YEAR-OLD FILLIES. These fillies are mature enough now to accept stallions and will often leave the band during their second summer.

YEARLINGS AND FOALS. The ranking of the youngsters in the band follows that of their dams. For example, the lead mare's foal and yearling will drink at the water holes first; then the others will step up in the order of their ranking.

The pecking order saves energy and eliminates confusion because, once it is in force, the horses will keep their places.

Otherwise, the members of the band would be in a constant power struggle. In times of crisis, the members don't have to waste time wondering who is giving orders. They instantly look to the lead mare; she tells them to follow her.

Wild to domestic; or from free to fenced

Horses in pastures follow this pattern: one horse is the leader, and the others are followers. Stallions, obviously, cannot be included with domestic arrangements. The horse with the most dominant personality will play the role of protector. A strong-willed mare or a bossy gelding will handle the position.

Our gelding Clip assumed that role immediately over Sierra when Clip moved in. He has remained in charge and insists upon eating and drinking first. If there is a loud crackle in the woods, he'll snort the danger honk and herd Sierra away to safety.

Lead horses take the job seriously, using kicks and bites to put any new horse in his place for trespassing on the band's property. The lead horse will also chase a newcomer. Clearly, the first reaction of the lead horse is not the equivalent of, "Hello, friend," but rather, "Get out of our pasture. Now."

Your horse is the unfortunate stranger and needs to be safeguarded after the quarantine period is over and it's time to join the other horses. This is best accomplished in gradual steps behind a strong fence.

In a letter, Canadian horse owner and columnist Thomas W. Brooks related the process he has followed with the Spider, his wise and locally celebrated Arabian gelding.

"The Spider has resided in four different stables in the ten years we've been together. With each move, he settled in easily; and in each case, he was kept separate, at least for an initial period…to see how things were going to shake out.

"I don't mean…that he was kept isolated in a stall away from others of his own kind, only that he was kept in a separate paddock…I'm a great believer in introductions being made over a fence first…When confronted, the less dominant animal will give

way, but if pursued aggressively while at the same time being confined by a fence, panic ensues, and…panic can lead to injury. In two of four locations, the Spider was confronted by aggression that set him in a panic mode. The only solution was not to paddock said horse and the Spider together."

These important observations underline the need for protection. Another factor involved in the introduction ritual is the equine reliance on scent. Horses will not trust anything new until they have a chance to breathe in the scent of it.

One experienced horsewoman I know, Loretto McCartney, frequently had to introduce new horses to the herd while she was working at a Thoroughbred breeding operation. The system the farm used was to enclose the herd in a small pasture with hay to eat and to let the new horse out in an adjoining paddock. The new horse would run until tired. Then, the handlers would remove him from the paddock and let the herd in. The new horse would be put into the small pasture with the hay. The herd would

Free no longer. These are wild horses soon after a roundup in Montana. Wild horses exhibit equine behavior in its purest form. In pastures, domestic horses will follow the same pattern of social interaction as their wild counterparts. Photo by Greg Albright, courtesy of the Bureau of Land Management.

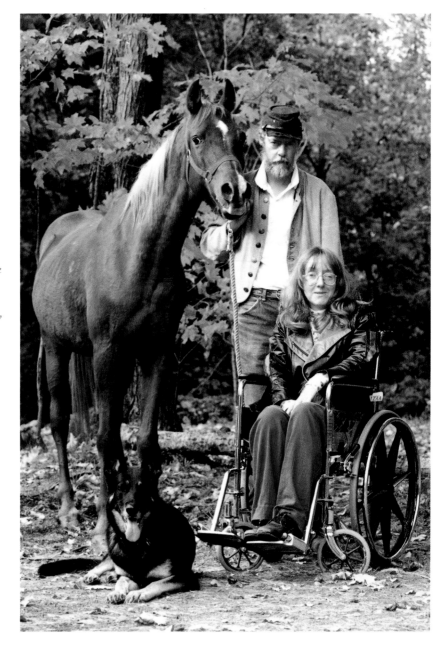

Newspaper columnist Tom Brooks and his horse, the Spider, have explored Canada's back roads and drive-in donut shops. They've experienced the ups and downs of changing stables several times. The Brooks family of Gravenhurst, Ontario: Tom, his wife, Marian, the Spider (the one horse in a one-horse town) and Ashley. Photo by Steve Mayes of Brampton, Ontario.

check out the scent of the manure left by the stranger, and the stranger would check out theirs.

McCartney explained, "If you let them get used to the smell of each other's bodies and manure before mixing, they calm down, and there is less violence when they meet. We also gave them plenty of time to sniff over the fence. When all was quiet, we mixed them, making sure they had a lot of space to maneuver in.

"Geldings were usually the easiest [to mix in]; the worst were the babies. They would run through fences to get away from the bullies because they just couldn't stop quickly enough to avoid the fence."

As you can see, horses need to be introduced carefully. When your horse is ready to meet the herd, try the process of switching the herd and your horse in the two paddocks. After you've accomplished this and your horse is alone, bring the other horses in one at a time. Give your horse the chance to get acquainted with each one before adding the next.

When meeting, horses will sniff noses and perhaps squeal and strike out with a front leg. This is normal and doesn't necessarily mean they will fight. There may be nips or kicks, but that should soon pass. Don't interfere unless it's getting too aggressive. Leave the halters on in case you need to remove a horse quickly.

Once the whole group is together, the scene will not be peaceful, but let them work it out. Since there is a new addition, each one in the group will now be battling the others as they readjust to their new place in the pecking order. Everything should be sorted out in a few days.

Fences make introductions safer.

This is a tense moment for a new horse. Will he be accepted or rejected?

Pasture problems and solutions

MARES AND GELDINGS. Many stables prefer to keep the mares in one pasture and the geldings in another. However, mares and geldings can coexist in compatible groups. The main factors are the horses' personalities and the ratio of males to females. Mixing several geldings and one mare is not a good idea because jealous conflicts will erupt when the mare comes in season. However, one gelding living with several mares can work out well.

Moving in for a closer look.

Other horses come
over to check out
the new one.

NUMBER OF HORSES. The more horses there are in a confined
territory, the more conflicts you will have. The greater the area,
the less pressure on everyone. The rule of thumb is at least two
acres per horse.

FEEDING IN GROUPS. Once again, the social ladder controls the
situation; the lead horse eats first. Horses are not too generous
about sharing their food. The best strategy for feeding grain in a
field is to use an individual bucket for each horse. Feed the most
dominant horse first; then, quickly feed the others in the order of
their ranking in the herd. Space out the buckets as far as you can.
For hay, put out more piles of hay than there are horses, so
everyone will get some. The horses will move from place to place
as if they are playing musical chairs.

In our pasture with two horses, I put out four piles of hay. Clip
eats at his favorite spot then checks out each pile to see which
one tastes the best. Sierra munches away at whatever pile he just
left. On cool autumn mornings when Clip is feeling frisky, he will
motor back and forth between the piles at a racing pace, just as he
used to do coming down the homestretch in his glory days on the
track.

This isn't going to be easy. Personality plays a role in how fast a horse will find his place in the herd.

PERSONALITY CLASHES. Once the introductory period is over, things generally settle down. However, sometimes horses develop a strong dislike for each other that goes beyond the daily jostling of nips and kicks. Eventually, the air may clear, and the horses will simply avoid each other. Some, though, will hold a grudge and deliver a swift hard kick or a chomp while passing by the object of their discontent. Separate the warriors; it is better than allowing one of the horses to receive a crippling injury.

THE BULLY. Some horses become bullies. The reasons may stem from chronic pain, chemical imbalance, or emotional resentment. The result is a serious problem for the horses around them. If the stable manager doesn't put him in another paddock, take action and remove your horse. If your horse is the troublemaker, consult a vet about tests to try and determine the cause. In any case, keep him separate for the safety of the herd.

Bullies tend to pick on the small and the weak. I once saw an extreme example of this. Four mares and two fillies were living in a large pasture. In the group were two very close friends, a Shetland pony, nine months pregnant, and a miniature horse named Whinny.

Every morning, the Shetland would wait by the gate until

Whinny came out. Then, they would walk to the far end of the pasture and graze side by side. During the afternoons, they would swish flies off each other with their long bushy tails.

One afternoon, a beautiful dapple-gray gelding, about 15 hands high, was put out in their pasture. Previously, the gray was used as a stallion, but he had been gelded about six months prior to this. He'd been turned out with other horses many times.

In the pasture, he immediately began racing around. The mares and fillies scattered. The gray gelding lowered his head and started herding them like a stallion with his band.

Suddenly, he made a beeline for the Shetland mare and Whinny. They got scared and started running faster. Their panic seemed to infuriate him, for he rushed up and viciously bit Whinny on the hindquarters. We watched in horror as he started to go for her neck, because stallions will seize and shake a predator's neck to kill it.

Whinny poured on what speed her little legs could muster, but it was too much for her. Her front leg gave way under the strain. When she bobbled and slowed, the gray gelding veered off. The

Horses in a panic to get away from a bully's aggression can be injured. Give the horses as much space as possible to allow them a chance to get out of harm's way. Photo by the author.

Shetland pony had been galloping some yards in front of Whinny, but now she turned around and came back, putting herself between Whinny and the gray.

Whinny came to a stop, her sides heaving with the exertion. The gelding circled, coming toward them again. But the Shetland was now standing guard in front of Whinny, with her ears flat back. Meanwhile, the gelding's owner was dashing across the pasture, shouting at him. Hearing his name seemed to bring him back to his senses, and he finally left the two friends alone.

The aftermath was that Whinny sprained a tendon and was lame for a long time, but she did recover. Two months later, the Shetland mare had a lovely little filly. When the mare and foal were turned back out in the pasture, Whinny seemed very happy to join them, and two friends became three.

Why the gelding suddenly attacked Whinny like that was a mystery. Perhaps it was a stallion herding instinct pushed too far by excitement, or the gray may have thought Whinny was a big dog. With her tiny size and shape, she did resemble a Saint Bernard dog at a distance.

Clearly, anyone can misjudge things. In the field next to our pasture, a wild deer once mistook our Golden Retriever for a wayward fawn. She saw him standing in the tall weeds and came over to investigate. He was scared to death and didn't move a paw as the doe came closer and closer. Finally, she realized her mistake and quietly walked away, much to our dog's relief!

THE ROMANTIC GELDING. As already noted, a gelding may believe he is still a stallion. When mares come into season, he could chase others away from them and attempt to mount his favorites.

You may not see this happen, but if your mare comes in with scrapes on the point of her hindquarters or bites and roughed up areas by her withers and neck, you should check to see if a gelding is responsible.

OUTCASTS. If after a few weeks with the group, your horse is still grazing by himself, the herd may be rejecting him. Some lead mares, however, will keep a new horse away from the herd for a month or more.

You could try turning out your horse in a small paddock with one quiet horse and see if they'll make friends. If you can't arrange to do this, see how it goes over the next couple of weeks. Some horses don't mind being independent, but if your horse acts lonely and depressed, seriously consider finding another stable.

If your horse is stabled at your farm, experiment by pairing horses in different paddocks. Maybe the new arrival will find a compatible horse. If that doesn't work, your horse might accept a goat, pony, or burro as a companion. Burros have such interesting personalities that a new burro could become a source of much needed fun.

Horse friendships

A number of factors determine how horses choose their friends. Understanding this can help you arrange the pairing of horses to promote pasture harmony.

- Status. Friends tend to be close to the same social ranking in the herd.
- Female bonding. A mare and her filly or two mares usually form the most affectionate friendships.
- Mares and geldings. These can form a tight bond. A sensitive

If problems arise, try different pairings of horses.

pair will graze together and nibble each other's itchy spots on their backs, withers, and necks. They can become distressed and even panicky if separated.

- Breed type. Similar breeds will often pair up, for example, two Thoroughbreds or two Mustangs. When horsewoman Robin Rivello adopted her wild horse, Reno, from the BLM (the Bureau of Land Management government program), she kept her at a boarding stable. Reno got along fine with the domestic horses. When another BLM filly arrived though, Reno seemed to know she was a Mustang and immediately befriended her.
- Stallions and mares. In the wild, some stallions have been observed being very affectionate to certain mares, even out of courting season. Other stallions simply treat all their mares like objects of personal property.

The nature of the stallion

When you see a stallion's raw power and surging instincts to reproduce, you're amazed he can be tamed at all. A stallion is strong and can be unpredictable. Anyone dealing with a stallion needs to be very experienced and to be in control.

Horse friendships can be very strong.

A stallion will respect a person who has a quiet and confident manner. A human who appreciates his pride and intelligence and who gives him a chance to be good will have a safe relationship with him.

Unfortunately though, people often expect the worst from a stallion. Therefore, they try to dominate the animal with threats and physical force before he does anything wrong. This can result in trauma and injuries to the stallion and the handler. The gentle methods of educating horses that authors such as Linda Tellington-Jones, Pat Parelli, GaWaNi Pony Boy, and Monty Roberts recommend can be very helpful.

Another serious consideration in the management of a stallion is keeping him in extended confinement. I once worked briefly with a prize Arabian stallion. He was so valuable that he was kept in a stall twenty-three out of twenty-four hours. Many days, he didn't go out at all. When he finally did go out, he was expected to be totally calm and rational while walking to his paddock. On the occasions when he wasn't, the handler would continually jerk the lead chain down on his nose.

It's unfair to sentence a horse to life imprisonment in the prime years of his life. Understandably, stallions need to be kept apart, but they should be able to see and hear other horses; other-

This magnificent Holstein stallion is handsome, sensible, and easily handled.

wise, they will become depressed. Stallions who are treated with respect and allowed plenty of exercise will benefit the future of the breed by leaving a legacy of emotionally stable fillies and colts.

The question of colts

Many foals named Surprise have resulted from low fences and cunning, springy colts. At the age of two, sometimes even as young as eighteen months, colts can reproduce.

I remember a stable that had a two-year-old Appaloosa colt named Tippecanoe. His owner assured all the boarders whose horses shared a pasture with him, "Don't worry about Tippy, he's too young to do anything."

The next spring, new foals kept appearing in the morning mist, wearing white Appaloosa spots on their little rumps. One mare, a gallant old Standardbred, had a beautiful Appaloosa filly the same day Apollo 11 came back from its historic moon mission. Her owner celebrated the event by calling her Splashdown.

To avoid surprise foals splashing down in your pasture, keep young lusty colts out of the paddock!

When stallions enjoy life, they will pass on robust mental and physical qualities to the next generation.

4

Stress Reducers

Moving a horse is a major upheaval that leaves lingering patterns of tension and stress in its wake. You'll need to address these issues to release the remaining insecurities and frozen fears that can show up as tense muscles and behavioral problems. Your goal in the first week is to help your horse feel safe again, so he can connect to you and to his new environment.

Horses under pressure

A horse worries with his entire mind and body. The way to help an anxious horse is to relax his body and to soothe his emotions. You must address both the physical and emotional aspects of stress because they are like a ping-pong ball, and you can't have the pong without the ping.

These are some signals that a horse is having trouble coping with the move:

AGITATED ACTIONS. Stall walking or pacing up and down the fence line are common; so are fretful whinnying and restlessness while being led or under saddle.

HOMESICKNESS. This feeling can evolve into depression if a horse continues to miss old friends and his former home. A

depressed horse will have a dull look in his eyes and a dejected expression. He'll keep his head lowered while standing in the stall or pasture. He may also move about in a listless, shuffling way. Since these symptoms could also indicate an illness, take his vital signs and report any abnormalities to your vet.

AGGRESSION. Some horses, instead of becoming withdrawn, will show their unhappiness by becoming overly aggressive and acting out. In their anger, they may kick or bite at the walls, people, or other horses.

DECREASED APPETITE AND WEIGHT LOSS. The horse may leave some or all of his grain or hay because of nervous tension or depression. Check the grain for mold and the hay for mustiness and thorns to be sure they are not the problem. Examine his teeth for sharp points that could cause him to avoid eating. Sharp points will need to be rasped by a vet or equine dentist. If the problem continues, you could have the horse examined by a vet for stomach ulcers.

ALLERGIC REACTIONS. When the immune system's defenses are lowered as a result of stress, the body becomes more susceptible to allergic reactions to chemical toxins, irritants such as fly spray, and air pollution. Signs of allergies include watery eyes, nasal discharge, itchy areas, labored breathing, and skin problems such as hives. Consult your vet for ways to relieve the horse's discomfort.

RESPIRATORY PROBLEMS. When the immune system is down, especially in young horses, colds and flu can take hold. Call the vet at once to discuss treatment. Veterinarians strongly advise that you never give antibiotics left over from another illness. Treatment needs to be tailored to the current situation.

OTHER POSSIBLE CAUSES. In addition to being upset because of problems associated with adjusting to a new environment, a horse may also show symptoms of anxiousness as a result of other problems.

Far left: Being a stranger in a stable is very stressful. Horses benefit from methods to release these anxious feelings and to relax tense muscles.

- Exercise. The horse may need to spend more hours in the pasture.
- Feed. Too much corn, grain, or alfalfa hay can produce edgy behavior. Reduce the ration and see what happens.
- Neighbors. Once the quarantine period is over and the horse is in with the herd, he may have trouble with his stablemates. Horses that don't get along will squabble. In adjoining stalls or paddocks, they may keep nipping at each other or kicking at the walls or fence. The continual tension is certainly stressful.

After you've administered any necessary medical care and adjusted his living arrangements, you might want to explore other ways to help with stress-related problems. The following sections contain brief overviews of various techniques used to relieve tension and to promote confidence.

Voice and the influence of sound

The human voice is one of the most effective instruments we possess to influence a horse. Because a quiet voice suggests nurturing and safety, it will have a calming effect.

Horses pay attention to the sound of a quiet voice.

My mare Sierra had been rounded up as a two-year-old during a rescue effort by the BLM to save some of the wild horses dying from drought conditions in Nevada. When our paths crossed, she had been in captivity for three years, but due to some rough experiences, she was still wary of humans.

To help her learn to trust me, I talked to her a great deal, just sitting near her in the paddock. She listened with keen attention, not because of my sparkling conversation, but because as a wild horse, she was determining the danger I posed to her. The softer the tone of voice I used, the more she let her defenses down. I was establishing that I was not a predator. Animals that stalk horses do not announce their arrival with their voice; rather, they approach and hunt in deadly silence.

Wildlife photographers and research scientists who encounter horses in the wild have recorded instances of horses reacting dramatically to the sound of their voices.

Journalist Hope Ryden related such an event in her book, *Wild Horses I Have Known*. Alone in the Nevada desert photographing Mustangs, Ryden was caught off guard by the abrupt appearance of a powerful gray stallion. He pranced and snorted about her with threatening gestures, even using the pre-fight ritual of pawing the ground.

Spending relaxed time together is fun and helps your horse develop trust in you.

She couldn't escape; running away was out of the question. She decided there was only one option: her voice. When she started speaking to him in a soothing tone, he perked up his ears. She kept up a friendly flow of talk and watched in amazement as his angry glare transformed into a curious stare.

Suddenly, he caught the scent of another stallion and band of mares moving over the ridge. In one swift burst of passion he neighed, wheeled about and galloped off towards the horses, much to Ryden's relief. Alone, unarmed, and faced with a wild angry stallion, the sound of her soft voice may have saved her life.

Tone

In the story above, it's apparent that the tone of voice you use with a horse can have a great effect on his reactions. Different tones carry different messages.

- Deep loud voice. This is threatening to a horse. It indicates that someone is aggressive and likely to inflict harm. It has the same effect as the menacing growl or bark of a dog. It is a clear warning to expect an attack.
- Harsh shout. This frightens a horse and should only be used in an emergency, for example, if the horse is doing something dangerous. It takes a horse a long time to fully trust you again after he hears you shout.
- High pitch. The friendly tone used for talking to babies is acceptable unless it's sharp, squeaky, or used too long.
- Gentle voice. This tone suggests, "All is safe, you can trust me. I won't lash out and hurt you."
- Hushing sounds. Drawn-out hushing sounds, like a quiet, deliberate, "Sh-sh-sh," work well to settle a horse. It gives him something on which to focus.

Breath

The signals made with inhaling and exhaling of breath command equine attention. Horses are acutely attuned to these sounds because they communicate with each other in this way. They will notice a sharp breath from a horse or person from up to twenty yards away.

When my horses are excited and acting flighty, I'll take a deliberate, deep breath, and exhale loudly to regain their attention. Most of the time, they will mirror the action, take a deep breath themselves, and start to settle down.

This makes sense in terms of equine survival tactics because horses take their cues from others. They watch the lead mare to see whether they should be alert for danger or relax and go back to grazing. It's important for wild horses not to expend more energy than is necessary. If they go running around for no purpose, they'll burn up energy that is hard to replace. On the range and in the deserts and mountains of the West, food can be scarce.

When you respect your horse's natural intelligence, you will both enjoy a much happier relationship.

Equine massage therapy

A sensitive use of the hands can release tension in the mind and body. However, as discussed here, massage is not about your treating muscle injuries, which should only be done by trained therapists or vets, but about relaxing the horse.

Before you begin, establish an attitude of respect for the horse's integrity and personal space. You should not assume that you can do whatever you want and your horse will accept it. That attitude creates resistance, and you want to reduce tension, not increase it.

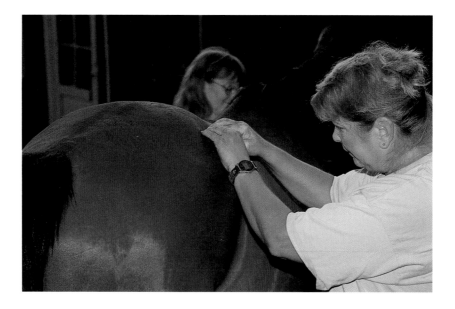

A therapy session with certified equine sports massage therapist Lyn Kamer.

Therefore, you should wait until the horse is comfortable with being touched before you begin. This basic courtesy can have far-reaching effects on your relationship and the results you achieve. Respect builds a bridge and opens the way for communication on many levels.

Maintain a positive attitude because your horse will take his cue from you as to whether this is something to enjoy or not. Lyn Kamer, a certified equine sports massage therapist, has worked on thousands of clients' horses ranging from barrel racers to dressage horses. She says, "Yes, my thoughts and mood have a definite effect on the horse. I generally focus on what I'm doing, and the horse will then relax and get into the massage. Some take longer than others."

There are times when you should not massage a horse. Kamer advises, "A new injury involving the soft tissue with associated heat and swelling should not be massaged, nor should you massage anything where a bone might be broken. You also need to be careful about working on a pregnant animal because of opening up acupoints that might have detrimental effects on the fetus."

Other occasions when it is best not to massage are when a horse has a fever, undiagnosed lumps, open wounds, influenza, heart disease, or cancer.

Basic massage

Here are several useful techniques to relieve muscle tension.

STROKING OR EFFLEURAGE. Make long gliding strokes with an open flat hand in the direction of the heart. This is beneficial because it aids the circulation of blood. Think of your strokes as a slow stream of water running down smooth rocks. Breathe deeply and steadily to create a tranquil atmosphere.

COMPRESSION. This involves pressing down with a flat hand into the fullest part of the muscle. Repeat this several times in a row. Slide further down the muscle and repeat. Compression is useful in releasing tight muscles, but avoid putting pressure on bones, the spinal column, and the lower half of the legs.

KNEADING OR PETRISSAGE. Use a motion like kneading dough. Lift up, lightly squeeze, and roll the skin and muscle. Be careful not to pinch the skin or to dig in with your fingernails. Petrissage increases the flow of tissue fluids and brings in additional oxygen.

RAKING MOVEMENT. Spread out your fingers like a garden rake and move across the chest and between the front legs. Go lightly from the withers area along the back to the tail. Always be extra careful near the hindquarters and keep an eye on the horse's mood.

Many therapists begin a session with effleurage strokes going down the horse's body from neck to shoulders, withers to elbow, and neck to back to hindquarters in the direction the hair grows. Once the horse relaxes into the motion and accepts the contact, you can introduce the kneading and compression. Another calming movement is to massage the crest of the neck, working from the withers to the poll, gently tugging on the mane by the ears.

With any of these techniques, start with a light pressure to see how the horse responds; then, increase by degrees. It's always better to be gentle rather than to be too strong. If the horse shrinks from your hand, the area may be tight or painful, so ease up. Be alert for other signals that the horse is getting defensive: head tossing, pawing, tail swishing, and foot stamping. If this happens, back off and go to a less sensitive area.

Horses react rapidly, so don't work in tight quarters. A box stall is usually big enough, but a standing stall is not. Leave the

Horses respond quickly to the right pressure.

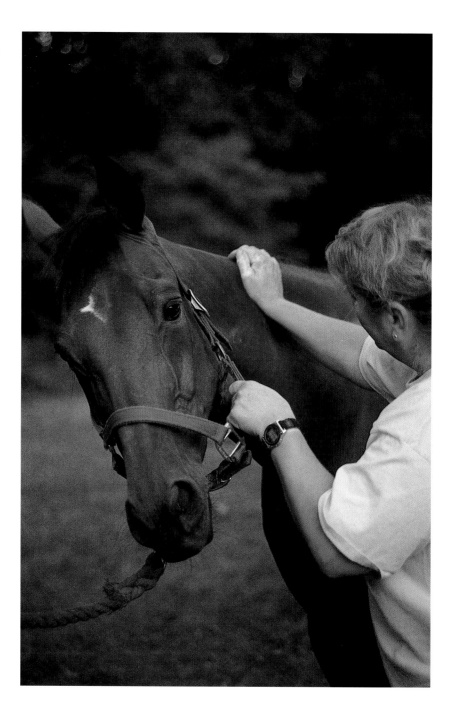

door latch open for ease in exiting. The main aisle in the barn is fine for working if it's not a busy thoroughfare.

If you can, have a helper hold the horse. If you don't have a helper, you can use cross ties, but a dangerous situation can arise if the horse startles and flies backward. You should only use cross ties if the horse is experienced with them and is sensible enough to stand quietly for a period of time.

Work with a sense of purpose and keep the sessions short, say ten to fifteen minutes, so the horse doesn't stiffen in resistance. Trust your hands and experiment with the techniques to see which one your horse enjoys the most.

Acupuncture

The ancient Chinese healing system of acupuncture employs extremely thin needles placed at specific points on the body. These points are linked to various organs, areas, and systems.

The object of inserting the needles is to unblock the flow of the life-force energy, called *chi* (pronounced "chee"), which flows along invisible paths in the body called meridians. When the chi is unblocked, the cycle of pain ends.

Acupuncture demands an in-depth knowledge of the location of the approximately 365 points. Only a veterinarian certified in acupuncture or a professional acupuncturist should administer acupuncture.

Horse owners frequently report good results from this therapy. Horses don't seem to mind the needles, and the improvement seen in various conditions can be very impressive. Of course, just like traditional medicine, it doesn't always work.

Acupressure

Acupressure addresses the same points on the body as acupuncture. The difference is that acupressure uses the hands rather than needles. The pressure of hands can bring healing and relief from tension; however, the results are usually not as effective or as rapid as acupuncture.

After learning the location of the points, you can do acupressure yourself. Many excellent books are available that explain in detail how to perform this therapy. While you are working, pay attention to the horse's reactions and body language. When the pressure makes him too uneasy, work on another area. Remember not to do any bodywork on pregnant mares because it could harm the unborn foal.

Both acupuncture and acupressure are used by trainers to help their horses overcome pain, deal with a lack of confidence, and cope with intense situations such as moving, showing, or racing. Since emotions and feelings are energy, these methods can assist in rebalancing the energy and can give the horse a comfortable sense of security.

During an interview, horsewoman Loretto McCartney spoke about the benefits she saw when these methods were used on horses recovering from track injuries and on mares arriving from other farms for breeding.

McCartney related that twice a month a veterinarian came and administered "acupuncture and acupressure, and showed me some therapeutic massage to complement her practices. It was really interesting to watch. When the horse was 'done,' the needles just fell out and hung there. It only took about twenty minutes to half an hour per horse, and the horses really seemed to benefit from it.

"The massage therapy certainly worked to relax some extremely high-strung race horses. [One dapple gray mare]…was like wood; her muscles were in a constant spasm, and her nerves would not allow her to relax or even lay down…. The doctor used acupuncture and acupressure once a month, and nightly I massaged and addressed the acupressure points on her body….The techniques really worked for her; you could feel the difference. Slowly, the wooden quality started to leave the muscles, and her stride changed and became lower and looser."

Chiropractic

Equine chiropractic practitioners believe that when the skeletal system and spinal column are out of alignment, the health of the whole body is affected. The misaligned vertebrae, known as subluxations, are adjusted back into place by the chiropractor's hands or by gentle taps with a rubber mallet.

Some symptoms that may indicate a horse has a subluxation include lameness, resistance to saddling and riding, hollowing the back and irritable actions when pressure is applied (this could also mean sore back muscles), any unusual posture when standing, refusal to jump in a formerly willing horse, and a tense stiffening of muscles when asked to do collection or lateral work under saddle.

Holistic vets, who believe in treating the mind, body, and spirit together, will often advise chiropractic work in conjunction with acupuncture and homeopathic and herbal remedies. Relieving the stress of any misalignments will definitely enable the horse to feel more at ease.

Herbal products

One peek in a supply catalog will reveal how many herbal remedies and feed additives are available commercially for calming horses. The herbs are sold as fresh or dried plants, in capsules, tinctures or alcohol extracts, in solutions mixed with water, oil, or glycerin, or as salves and poultices.

Additives for quieting a horse's behavior are offered in a variety of forms including paste, pellet, and liquid. The ingredients usually include the herb valerian, the amino acid tryptophane, thiamine or vitamin B1, and magnesium.

Valerian is an effective herb for reducing tension. However, in many states it is banned from use for racehorses and performance horses. Be careful with this herb around cats because it can induce severe vomiting in them.

Using supplements and herbal products without a precise

knowledge of their action can be harmful. Many veterinarians are becoming concerned about the misuse and overuse of these substances. Anything added to a horse's system causes a reaction in his body, sometimes upsetting a delicate balance. For example, the liver is the body's toxin cleanser. It must work extra hard to clear the system of any overdoses of nutrients or foreign matter. Carefully consider the results of using supplements and consult your vet for advice before giving your horse any of these products.

Homeopathy

The field of medical treatment known as homeopathy was developed in the eighteenth century by the innovative physician Dr. Samuel Hahnemann (1755–1843) of Germany. His experiments with quinine for treating malaria led him to theorize that "like cures like." The principle involved is similar to vaccination. Tiny amounts of a substance that can cause a disease or certain symptoms are used to stimulate the body to fight and resist the disease. This reaction brings the body into balance, leading to a cure or to an easing of the symptoms.

Convinced of the potential of his discovery, Hahnemann went on to develop over 2,500 homeopathic remedies using various substances from plants to animal products. His remedies were extensively tested on the battlefield in 1813. He had a phenomenal rate of success, curing 178 out of 180 cases of typhoid.

At the present time, the international interest in complementary fields of medicine has led to a resurgence in the popularity of homeopathy. However, a homeopathic veterinarian should select the appropriate remedy to avoid harming the horse as a result of using the wrong remedy or from giving an overdose.

Flower essences

In the early years of the twentieth century, Dr. Edward Bach, a physician who held surgical and medical posts in London, devised useful remedies from the essences of thirty-eight different flowers. Dr. Bach discovered that the essences directly address the emotional state. He targeted the emotions because he believed fear and negative feelings were responsible for the majority of illnesses and diseases.

Although he developed the flower solutions for human use, they were found to be equally effective with animals. Because they are very concentrated, only a few drops are needed for a treatment. The remedies can be put in the horse's feed or drinking water (several drops in the feed or ten drops in a bucket of water). They can be placed on a carrot or on the tongue or gently rubbed on the gums. Remedies can also be sprayed on the horse or around his living area.

Dr. Bach named the remedies after the flowers they are made from such as honeysuckle, holly, and cherry plum. Mixtures of several flowers are also available; a very popular one is called Rescue Remedy. This remedy can help horses calm down and regain their senses after serious injuries, accidents, and traumatic events.

On a farm I once visited, I saw a gelding come in from the field with a horrendous, gaping wound on the gaskin of his leg. Understandably, he did not want to stand still for the vet. After being given Rescue Remedy, the gelding settled down in a few minutes. The vet was then able to stop the bleeding and suture the horse's leg.

Another advantage of these remedies is that there are no negative side effects as occurs with herbs, additives, or drugs. Since flower essences work by affecting the emotional state, they are very useful for horses dealing with insecure feelings resulting from new surroundings.

In her book, *Complete Holistic Care and Healing for Horses*, Mary Brennan, D.V.M. says, "I often suggest Bach Flower Remedies to help with a sensitive horse's adjustment when he is moved to a new stable."

Aromatherapy

Aromatherapy is the ancient practice of using the scent of essential plant oils to provide physical and emotional assistance. This therapy can be very effective in situations that provoke stress, fatigue, and anxiety. Scent can trigger strong responses, for it directly affects the part of the brain that deals with emotions and memory.

Since horses have a highly complex sensory system, they actively respond to the use of aromatherapy. One friend of mine observed a very agitated stallion thrashing about in a portable stall at a big arena event. After an herbalist applied some aromatherapy product on the walls of the stall, the horse calmed down in a matter of minutes.

Using this same idea, you can make a stall in a new location more inviting to your horse by sprinkling some essential oils around the perimeter. It is also helpful to sprinkle some in the trailer before you load your horse. This is especially useful for horses that do not trailer well, because it helps them to be more content during transport.

The essential oils are usually sold in dropper bottles in a pure form or diluted with another oil such as extra virgin olive oil, sweet almond oil, or grapeseed oil. The drops can be put on a cloth and inhaled or used in a vaporizer, but they should not be given by mouth. When diluted, you may use them in a compress or poultice. Don't mix the oils together. Some can have a powerful effect, so start with the smallest amount possible; begin with one or two drops.

Most health food stores carry these oils. They can also be purchased through mail-order supply companies listed in health magazines or on the Internet. You may have to experiment to find the exact product that works best for your horse, depending upon his individual needs. Some of the oils commonly used to alleviate anxiety and stress are frankincense, lavender, lemongrass, and patchouli: for depression, rose, sandalwood, neroli, and ylang ylang are used.

Animal Communication

Another resource to consider in helping your horse feel better is an animal communicator. Thoughts and emotions continually travel between horses and humans, but we only tend to take notice of our horse's gestures and body language.

Animal communicators can receive direct messages of how an animal is feeling mentally and physically from the animal itself. They can hear the animal's thoughts in their mind and feel a fleeting sensation of pain in their body where the animal is uncomfortable.

Scientists cannot stamp a definitive, "Yes, this is true," on animal communication because telepathy, intuition, and psychic awareness are involved. These are not things you can see or touch. However, you can validate the communication by the results that follow.

In many cases, when the animal tells the communicator the root cause of a behavioral problem or pinpoints the exact location of a physical injury, the vet can successfully treat the right area, or the problem behavior goes away without further effort.

Many animals show their appreciation that someone cared enough to ask what was bothering them, and they become more affectionate.

One of the leading pioneers in animal communication is Penelope Smith. Formerly a counselor for humans, Smith discovered that the methods that helped people worked as well and usually faster with animals.

In her book, *When Animals Speak*, Smith describes a consultation with a dressage horse that had been acting up. The horse explained to her through telepathy and images that the problem was a sore back. When Smith felt his back, she found a painful spot where the vertebrae were compressed. She told him that was where the trouble was and what to do about it. He rounded his back, and everyone standing by heard the vertebrae pop back into place.

The horse then told her he wanted to roll to release his spine. "He felt he had been working too hard, tensing his spine when trying to execute the dressage movements. His handler led him out to a good rolling area, where he thoroughly enjoyed himself. Later, when ridden, he moved smoothly and comfortably."

Another professional animal communicator, Anita Curtis, helps animals and their human companions through consultations in person and on the telephone. During an interview, Curtis shared some insights from her experience that are helpful in preparing horses going to a new stable.

"Before a horse is moved, the owner should tell him two things: why he is being moved and exactly what the new place looks like. Describe all the details, such as there's a brown board fence, a window in the stall. [Describe] how big the stall is and how many other horses are there. The worst thing horses face is the fear of the unknown. If you explain everything to them, when they come in they'll recognize the new location, walk right in, and settle down.

"At one barn, there was a young stallion being sent to another farm for training. During a consultation, I told him exactly what the place was going to look like. I got the return message from him, 'Well, when I get there and get off the trailer, I shall rear up high on my hind legs to show them who I am.'

"The owner of the horse didn't believe in animal communication, and when he heard this statement, he thought it couldn't have come from his horse because he never reared up.

"When they got to the training barn, they unloaded the stallion. He looked around and followed them meekly into the barn, and then he went straight up and walked around on his hind legs. When he plopped down, he was fine and didn't do it again. He just had to show them who he was!

Anita Curtis and her lovely Arabian mare, Legend's Desire. Photo courtesy of Anita Curtis.

"If you're buying or selling a horse, it's always a good idea to explain why.

Ponies go through a rough time when their riders outgrow them. They'll say to me, 'But I have always been so good, and I've always tried so hard.'

"The best thing you can do for ponies is to explain, 'You've been so wonderful to our child, and now we're going to ask you to move on and help to train another child.'"

For a horse having trouble adjusting to a move, Curtis recommends using a few drops of Rescue Remedy (one of the Bach Flower Essences) in the water or in the feed. Another thing that helps is to tell the horse how long he'll be staying there.

"Sometimes," Curtis says, "they've been through a couple of auctions, and they are afraid they are at a sale barn. You have to tell them, 'This is your new home, and this is where you are going to be.' However, if they are there for a couple of months for training, tell them how many times the moon will be in a certain phase. Say, 'You're going to be here when the moon is full, and then it will change. When it is full again, that's when you are going home.' They understand that.

"When communicating with horses, avoid using negative words such as 'never,' 'don't,' and 'can't' because there is no picture image for those words, and animals think in pictures. On the other hand, if I tell you, 'Don't think of a navel orange' what are you going to think of? It is best not to say things like, 'Don't

worry, nobody's going to hurt you,' because they will only hear, 'Worry, somebody's going to hurt you.'

Everything will be all right.

"Instead of telling a horse, 'You will never leave here,' try 'You will stay here. We will keep you healthy, and we will take care of you.'"

And what do horses ask when they find out they are moving?

Curtis says, "They always want to know if their friends can come and how much grass they are going to get."

If you haven't encountered animal communication before, it can be hard to believe it is really coming from the animals. However, once you give it a chance and start really talking to them, they will show you in a hundred ways that they understand. The proof will certainly open exciting new possibilities for you and your horse.

5 Your Support Team

The bay horse galloping along the fence line was eagerly watching his companions running in the far field. Unfortunately, when he reached the corner, he couldn't stop in time, and he slammed into the fence. As he wheeled around, I saw the blood streaming down his right front leg.

The stable manager made an emergency call to the vet; within twenty minutes, the bay's wound was being sutured. The cut involved an artery, which could have caused serious bleeding.

Respect for the time and expertise of professionals is vitally important to your horse's health and well-being. If "it takes a village to raise a child," then it takes a crew of knowledgeable people to care for a horse: the veterinarian, farrier, equine dental technician, stable manager, hay supplier, and horse sitter.

You need to build and maintain good relationships with the professionals who help you care for your horse. In the following sections, you'll find suggestions on how to do this.

The veterinarian

Obviously, courtesy is always appreciated whether you want to schedule regular appointments for examinations and vaccinations or you just need to ask for help with minor problems.

A spirited stallion galloping just for his own pleasure.

VACCINATIONS. Before you call, check your health records to see what your horse needs. Your horse requires many different types of vaccinations. He may need a vaccination particular to your area or to the location where you are showing. Explain what you want so your vet will have the vaccine on hand.

ADVANCE NOTICE. If you have a target date, say a horse show a month away, and you need a Coggins test, call at least two to four weeks in advance. This allows the vet time to fit you into his or her schedule. It also gives the horse time to recover from the effects of any inoculations before the event.

SEASONAL RUSH. Spring and summer are the busiest times because they are the foaling and horse show seasons. Allow extra time in scheduling an appointment and be flexible if your vet has to change the appointment.

PAYMENT. If you are consulting a vet for the first time, when you make the appointment, ask when and how the vet prefers to be paid. For example, will the vet bill you or should you expect to write a check before he or she leaves?

TELEPHONE CONSULTATIONS. Avoid calling the vet at dinner-time or very late at night unless it is for a true emergency or for foaling concerns. State the symptoms and the problem as clearly as possible. Give a brief account of how it happened; don't hold back any details because of embarrassment. This could affect the vet's advice on what to do until he or she arrives.

NOTES. In a serious situation such as colic, keep a written record of the horse's symptoms and vital signs every hour. This will be valuable information for your vet.

TROUBLE AHEAD. Tell the vet if your horse is troublesome or dangerous during examinations. When forewarned, the vet can allow extra time, bring the appropriate tranquilizer, and arrange for an assistant to help.

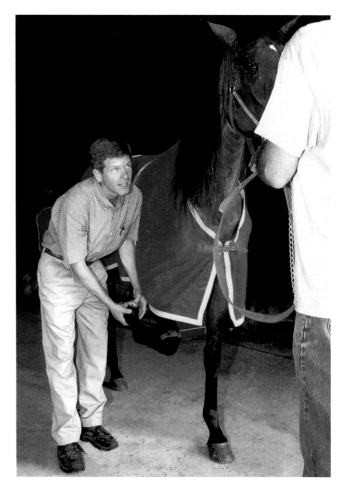

The indispensable veterinarian.

Day of the appointment

Consult an equine medical book and read about your horse's problem, so you'll know what questions to ask. You'll also have a better understanding of what the vet is telling you and the treatment options available. If you don't understand a medical term or procedure, ask the vet to explain it to you.

PREPARE FOR THE APPOINT-MENT. The horse should be in his stall with his halter on at the appointed time. Be forgiving if the vet is late. Most vets make an honest effort to arrive on time, but unforeseen problems can cause delay.

BE PRESENT. If your horse lives at a boarding stable, let the manager know right away when the vet is coming. If at all possible, be there to hold your horse. Your presence will reassure your horse and comfort him during inoculations and unpleasant examinations.

RECAP THE SITUATION. Vets see many clients each day and may not recall every detail about your horse. Briefly state the horse's background and any problems or symptoms. However, while the vet is listening to the heartbeat and counting breaths for respiration rates, be quiet so he or she can get an accurate count.

PAY ATTENTION TO YOUR HORSE'S BODY LANGUAGE. Horses are normally on edge around the vet, so keep a sharp eye on all your horse's reactions and gestures. Be on the alert to shorten the lead rope to keep him still or to warn the vet if the horse is threatening to kick or bite.

ASK QUESTIONS. Ask the vet about anything that concerns you, including the treatment. If it is complicated, ask for written instructions since it's easy to forget details. A research study showed that people only retain about twenty percent of the information that doctors give them.

DON'T INDULGE IN THE BUY-ONE-GET-ONE-FREE SYNDROME. It's not fair to ask the vet to look at another horse "as long as you're here." The vet is on a strict schedule, and the extra twenty minutes it takes to look at that other horse, goat, sheep, or pig throws off the rest of the day's appointments.

INQUIRE ABOUT THE PRICE OF PROCEDURES. Ask the cost of any specific treatments the vet may recommend. You'll want to know the cost before you give the go-ahead; otherwise, you might be shocked when the bill comes in the mail.

PAY THE BILL PROMPTLY. If you can't afford to pay all at once, ask your vet if you can arrange a payment plan.

WATCH YOUR HORSE AFTER THE VET LEAVES. If your horse received vaccinations, stay nearby for at least fifteen to thirty minutes in case your horse develops a reaction, for example, a hot, painful swelling at the site. Report this to your vet immediately.

BE LOYAL. When your horse is being treated for something and you're not happy with the results, don't just call in another vet. Talk to your vet first and ask for further ideas or ask for a recommendation for a second opinion. If you consult another vet without notifying your own vet first, you could find yourself dropped from his or her client list. Other vets may then be hesitant to help you.

Emergencies

Learn the clinical signs of illness so you know what is abnormal and what needs immediate action. When you call the vet, state your name and phone number first so you don't forget in the excitement. State the problem exactly along with your evaluation of its severity: bleeding, colic, bad accident, etc. Report the vital signs if you have them, where the horse is now, and how he's acting. Ask about any first-aid measures that you should attempt.

In an emergency, never give the horse tranquilizers or painkillers unless the vet specifically instructs you to do so. On arrival, the vet needs to know the horse's exact condition in order to diagnose and treat him properly.

Dangerous situations that justify an emergency call include:

- Colic.
- Laminitis.
- Profuse bleeding. This is defined as ¼ cup or more per minute.
- Anaphylactic shock (This is a severe and sudden allergic reaction. Symptoms may include: rearing up and collapsing, blue gums, swelling of the throat, hives, and labored breathing. A symptom can occur within one minute of an injection and can be fatal if untreated. The vet should have epinephrine on hand

for treatment. Horse owners, however, should not administer this drug because an incorrect dose could kill the horse.)

- Suspected poisoning.
- Acute diarrhea.
- Choking.
- Fever over 104 degrees F.
- Snakebite or bite from a suspected rabid animal.
- Eye injuries or infections.
- Puncture wounds or a wound that is swollen, hot, and infected.
- Refusal or inability to get up.

A horse that exhibits good manners while being shod or trimmed is a relief and a delight for the farrier.

While you're waiting for the vet, it may be difficult to stay calm, but try to for your horse's sake. During stressful situations, saying rhyming words in a slow rhythm can help you both breathe easier and recover some control.

The farrier

Most horse people treasure good farriers because of the extreme importance of their work. They are the doctors of equine locomotion. You should be a polite and grateful client.

When your horse's hooves need trimming or shoeing, call for an appointment at least two weeks in advance. However, a better idea is to set up a regular appointment schedule for every six to eight weeks. Hooves grow faster in the summer, so they will need more frequent care, possibly every four to five weeks.

If you are calling a farrier for the first time, be sure to ask whether you should expect to pay immediately or whether you will receive a bill in the mail. If your horse is difficult to shoe, let the farrier know so that he can allow extra time.

Preparation

EXERCISES. Practice all the actions your horse will use with the farrier: balancing on three legs, stretching the front and hind legs forward, placing a hoof between the knees, holding the hoof up for longer than usual, and lightly tapping on the hoof to get him used to the sound and feel of the hammer.

WORKING AREA. Find a clean, level, quiet place for the farrier to work. Select a spot away from other horses. A horse might reach over and sneak in a nip while your horse is standing for the farrier.

Day of the appointment

RIDE OR TURN OUT YOUR HORSE BEFORE THE APPOINT-MENT. This takes the nervous edge off, so he will be more content to stand still for a while.

READINESS. Your horse should be waiting in a stall or small paddock with his halter on at the appointment time. Brush off any mud on his legs and hooves.

DOGS. Remove all dogs from the area where the farrier will be working. Dogs love to chew on hoof trimmings, but their presence is an annoyance to the horse and the farrier. In addition, the dog might be kicked.

CONTROL. Stand with your horse during the appointment. If you can't be there, find someone to fill in for you. Your job is to control your horse and keep him calm. You can do this by entertaining him. If he starts getting bored or restless, lightly scratch his favorite spot such as on the chest, under the mane, or between the eyes.

Exercise before the appointment can help your horse be more willing to stand still.

Dogs need to be contained when the farrier is working. Photo by the author.

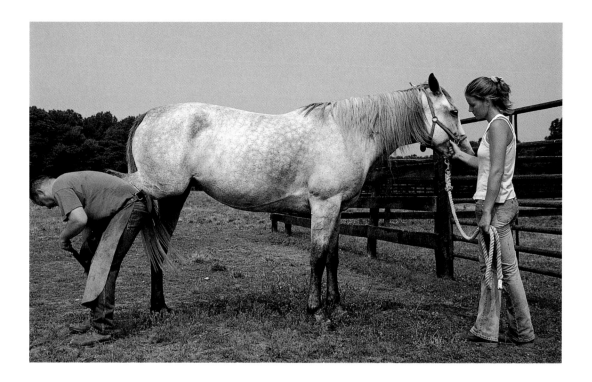

Holding your horse for the farrier is an important and pleasant task.

DANGER SIGNS. Warn the farrier if your horse is showing any signs of anger. Take care of it and remind your horse to behave before his behavior deteriorates.

LEAD ROPE. Keep your horse on a short lead, not so tight that he resists and pulls back, but short enough so that he can't sniff or slobber on the farrier's head or back. A horse's head is heavy. As he moves it around, he has to rebalance his weight; eventually, he ends up leaning on the farrier. This is very irritating to the farrier, and it's also hard on his or her back muscles.

FLY SEASON. Horses will stamp their front and back hooves to chase flies, and this could injure the farrier. Spray the horse with insect repellant ahead of time. Some farriers carry along a device that looks like a horse's tail; the person holding the horse can use it to brush away flies.

ACTIVE TAIL. If your horse is swishing his tail to chase flies away, the farrier could be in danger. Tail hair is thin and can slice a human eye. During fly season, have a friend hold the tail to the side while the farrier is working on the hind legs. If no one is available to help, you can tie the tail in a mud knot.

Equine dental technician

Dental care for horses is often neglected, but it is as important as regular farrier work. Horses should have their teeth examined every six months. At the very least, they need to receive dental care once a year.

The constant grinding action of the molars can create sharp edges that cut the tongue and the insides of the cheeks. A horse that keeps tossing his head or evading the bit may be experiencing pain from injuries in his mouth. The most common problem areas are the outer section of the upper row of molars and the inner edge of the lower row of molars.

Check your horse's teeth regularly; enjoy that crocodile smile!

The equine dental technician, commonly known as the dentist, will use a rasp to float, or file down, the sharp edges of the teeth. Specially trained veterinarians can also perform dental procedures.

Preparation for a dental appointment

There are several things you can do ahead of time to help your horse get ready.

Equine dentist Scott Gager, whose father, Ed Gager, is the author of *Sound Mouth, Sound Horse*, recommends that you "get the horse

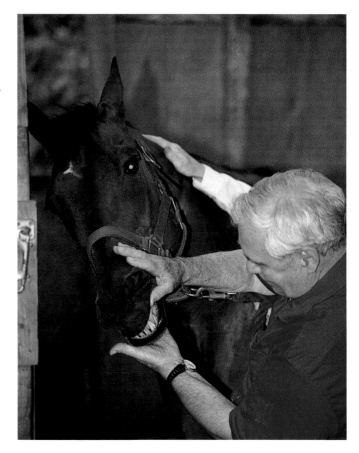

used to having a person's hands in his mouth. Carefully place your thumbs in and move them around on the gums." Wetting your hands with warm water first will make it more comfortable for the horse.

Also, practice opening the horse's mouth. To do this, lay your fingers on the horse's lips by the corners of the mouth. Jiggle your fingers, then slide them in through the space between the incisors and premolars—the interdental space. Horses will usually open their mouths when they feel this pressure. Be very careful with your fingers. Horses have been known to bite hard enough to amputate a finger.

For at least a week before the visit, young horses should receive daily basic grooming and handling lessons such as those described. Pay close attention when handling colts and fillies because they tend to be high spirited and unpredictable, and their reactions can be dangerous.

Take a few minutes a day to handle the horse and get him used to mouth work. It can save you and the dentist a lot of problems.

This horse is having his teeth floated to remove sharp hooks and points by a veterinarian specializing in equine dentistry. The speculum holds the mouth open so the vet can reach all of the horse's teeth.

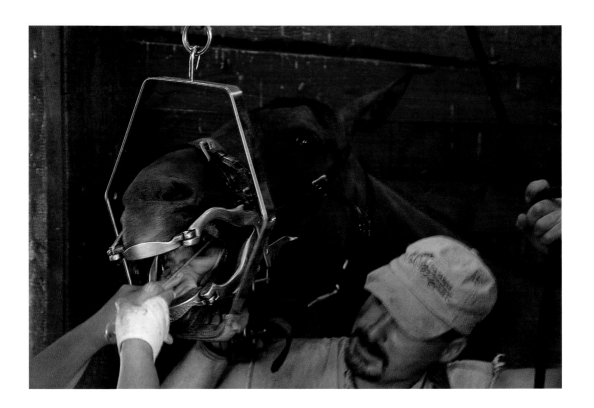

Signs of tooth trouble

- Slow chewing.
- Drooling.
- Quidding. Chunks of half-chewed hay will fall out of the mouth or get stuck between the cheek and teeth.
- Feed. Grain will drop out of the mouth while he's eating. Sometimes, the horse doesn't finish all his grain even though he's acting hungry and eager to eat.
- Head tilt. The horse will tilt his head to the side while chewing. This indicates pain in the teeth.
- Wounds on the tongue or inside the cheek.
- An unpleasant odor in the mouth or nostrils. The odor can be caused by diseased teeth.
- Weight loss.

Since horses' teeth keep growing throughout their lives, every age group needs regular dental checkups and care. Young horses and seniors require more frequent examinations.

We know about the teething problems of puppies and their need to chew. Yet it is easy to forget that up until the age of five, horses have a problem with teething as well.

If you are having training troubles with a horse in this age range, investigate his dental condition.

The stable manager is a V. I. P., a very important person to you and your horse.

Stable Manager

When you board your horse at a stable, the manager sees to your horse's care and comfort. In your absence, the manager is responsible for daily handling and will be the first to notice signs of ill health or lameness.

Running a stable is a difficult job with long hours, so acknowledge the manager's help with respect and gratitude. Here are some ways to be a welcome addition to the stable community.

BILLS. Pay your monthly board on time.

APPOINTMENTS. Try to coordinate your routine vet and farrier visits with other boarders to lessen the confusion of so many appointments at different times. In addition, the bill is usually less expensive if several boarders share the vet and farrier's call charge. Inform the manager well in advance about any upcoming appointments, especially if you cannot be there and need someone to hold your horse.

STALL CARD. Write down all your horse's feeding requirements, supplements, and medications on a stall card. In addition, note

Give a copy of your horse's medical records to the stable manager.

what your horse is allergic to and any information that someone unfamiliar with him needs to know for feeding or handling. Place the card where it can easily be seen but away from the reach of horse lips.

WARNINGS. Explain to the manager any negative habits your horse has, such as crowding the person leading him out. If your horse doesn't like a certain horse, mention it so that no one puts them out together.

WHOOPS. Report any damage your horse does, such as break a fence rail, and offer to pay for a replacement.

TODDLERS. Keep an eye on small children. Don't let them wander unattended or expect the manager to entertain them while you're riding.

RETURN THE FAVOR. Offer to watch over the horses on occasion. If the manager is going to an event, for example, and would have to rush back for the evening feed, lend a hand and feed the horses. Such assistance is always appreciated.

Hay

Horses love fresh grass, but hay is a staple for most horses twelve months a year. Although hay is expensive, trying to economize by buying hay at the low end of the price scale is a waste of money. Horses usually don't like the taste, and poor quality hay can compromise their health. Chronic respiratory problems, such as heaves, and colic can develop from eating dusty or moldy hay. Bales containing thorns, sticks, and weeds pose another risk to your horse.

No matter what price you pay for hay, always shake out the flakes and inspect the hay before giving it to your horse. I've found roadside trash, smashed and ragged soda cans, bread bags, candy wrappers, cup lids, torn pieces of tire rubber, and loose pieces of

baling wire in expensive hay. In cases such as this, contact your supplier and ask for replacement bales or your money back.

Before you call to buy hay, learn about the different varieties available in your area and what type is best for your horse. You'll be prepared then to know exactly what kind to purchase. You don't want a delivery of alfalfa when you need timothy.

If you've ever thrown thirty bales of hay off a truck, carried them in, and stacked them up, you can understand that it feels like you've run the Boston Marathon in a dust storm of prickly stickers. Clearly, sending the hay back will spark a lot of resent-ment!

Contacting the hay supplier

If you do the ordering for your horse's hay, you want to maintain good relations with your supplier.

PLAN AHEAD. Call the supplier three weeks before running out of your current stock of hay. This makes it easier to put you on the delivery schedule. It's important for your horse's sake, too, because you'll need to gradually mix in the new hay with the old, even if it is the same type of hay.

SEASONS OF SHORT SUPPLY. The supply of hay can run low during the winter and in the early spring before the new bales arrive. Keep this in mind as you make your plans. The prices will be higher in the winter, too.

DELIVERY WOES. Before delivery, warn the contact person about places on your farm to avoid driving a heavy truck. For example, if there has been a heavy rain and the ground is soggy in front of your barn, call that morning to tell them. If the hay truck gets stuck in the mud, you may never see that truck rumbling up your lane again.

PRICES. Most suppliers have a set price for a bale, and that's that. Bargaining with them is usually not an option. If you don't

Far left: Hay is life to horses. Choose it well.

want the hay, they will gladly sell it to someone else. Ask if there's a delivery charge. Also ask about the preferred method of payment: cash on delivery, prepayment, or charge.

ON ARRIVAL. Make sure the price per bale quoted on the phone is the same price you pay when it is delivered; innocent mistakes happen. If you are reasonable about it, there shouldn't be any problem.

The horse sitter

We all need a break now and then. If your horse lives with you, those breaks are almost nonexistent. The care of your horse while you are on vacation is a major concern. It's hard to enjoy your trip while worrying if your horse is being fed or being turned out into the pasture.

You'll want to have a horse sitter for vacations and in case something comes up at work or school. If you can't reach home in time to bring the horses in for the night or a sudden thunderstorm rolls into town hours before you can leave work, a quick call to a horse sitter could solve the problem.

Locating a horse sitter

You can usually find advertisements for horse sitters on bulletin boards at tack shops, at feed stores, and in vet offices. Your vet or farrier might be able to make a recommendation; you can also ask other horse owners if they know someone who cares for horses. These are some websites on the Internet that can help put you in touch with horse sitters:

■ The Horse Sitters - www.backeastfarm.com/horsesitters.html
■ The National Association of Professional Pet Sitters - www.petsitters.org
■ The Pet Sitters International - www.petsit.com

Ask the horse sitter to come over several days before you leave in order to meet your horse and go through the routine.

BEFORE THE SITTER COMES. Write down detailed instructions for feeding, care, and handling so the sitter has everything in writing. This helps clarify your own thoughts, too.

Note the amounts of grain and hay, any supplements, and where to locate the feed in case different types of hay are stored in different areas.

If your horse has any

"What? You need a vacation from me?" Horse sitters enable you to have a necessary break from the relentless daily chores of horse care.

behavioral habits, such as always rolling on the ground after he's turned out, note them so the sitter doesn't worry that your horse has colic. Describe how long he usually stays in the paddock, the hours when he goes out, and when he comes in. Horses are focused on their routines and become upset with any major changes.

Include the following telephone numbers:

- Where you can be reached day and night.
- Someone else who knows your horses, such as a family member or neighbor, in case you're out of reach and a problem arises.
- Your veterinarian, equine emergency clinic, and the farrier.
- Local police and fire department.
- A horse transportation company or friend with a horse trailer who would be willing to take your horse to an emergency vet clinic.

When the horse sitter visits

Allow plenty of time for the horse sitter to become acquainted with your horse and other pets in a relaxed atmosphere. Show him or her where the pitchforks are kept, the area to dump the manure, how the gates are latched, and whether you want the barn doors and windows left open or closed at night.

Give the sitter a copy of the written instructions, so he or she can ask any questions in the days before you go. Leave another copy of the instructions in the barn or house where they can be easily seen.

Go over the routine and explain the order in which the horses are fed to keep things as normal as possible. Tell the sitter the order the horses are used to going in and out of the barn. My gelding Clip gets upset when he has to wait and go second; then, he's a handful to walk outside. Otherwise, when he goes out first, he walks like a gentleman.

Give the sitter a copy of your horse's medical records, normal baseline vital signs, and current notes of any ongoing health problems. In your absence, these records could give the vet valuable information for diagnosis.

Work out the exact price to be paid and the fees for any extra work such as caring for other pets. This avoids bad feelings afterward about the bill. Be generous. A little extra encourages a willingness to come back and help you again.

Let your neighbors know that you're using a horse sitter. If they are forewarned, they won't suspect a thief and call the police when they see a strange car parked in your driveway or someone wandering around.

As a further precaution, since unsavory people may notice you are absent from your property, photograph your horse from several angles: front, back, and side views. Get close-ups of any distinguishing marks such as stars, stripes, snips, and socks. Photographs are useful for identification and insurance purposes in case of theft. Take some pictures of your tack as well. While you are away, keep your saddle in a safe place in the house.

Experienced horse sitters are valuable resources when you must be away from home. Many are skilled with other animals as well. Photo by the author.

Fire safety

You don't want to think about a stable burning and horses perishing, but these things happen. Fire safety statistics indicate that there are approximately 4,700 stable fires yearly in the United States. I remember the devastation when Garden State Race Track in New Jersey burned down. The news reports of horses being trapped in burning stables and horses fleeing the flames were awful. Close friends have lost beloved horses to barn fires, too.

Take steps to reduce the risk of barn fires:

- Put the telephone numbers of the police and fire departments in well-lit places in the house and barn.
- Do not permit smoking in or near the barn or where the hay is stored.
- Exercise care with electrical appliances. These are the biggest culprits behind stable fires. Avoid using space heaters. Be very careful when operating electric dryers because the lint is flammable. Unplug all appliances and radios when not in use.
- Have the wiring checked by an electrician every six months to a year. Inspect wires for rodent damage and age cracks. Wiring in stables should be encased in a conduit to prevent rodents from chewing through wires. Light bulbs in the stalls need to be in wire cages to prevent horses from breaking them with their heads. Make sure the bulbs are placed away from any holes in the roof. Dripping rain can short them out, causing a potential problem.
- Hot hay, smoldering shavings, and manure piles can ignite. Heat created by decomposing material can spark a blaze. When there's no air to draw off the heat, the material keeps getting hotter and eventually can start a fire. Store newly cut hay with space between the bales and in an area away from the barn. Check all the new bales for heat for at least a week after you bring them in. Fires often ignite in new bales several days after being stacked. If you find a hot one, turn the hose on it. Dispose of it afterward because wetting it will cause the hay to

Install numerous fire extinguishers in key locations throughout your barn and be sure everyone knows how to operate them.

mold. Store shavings away from the barn; monitor the manure pile closely. If you see the manure pile smoking, wet it down and break apart the smoking area to let air in. This helps to dissipate the heat.

- Buy the dry chemical variety of fire extinguishers and learn how to use them. If a blaze erupts, call the fire department first. Then, if the fire is in a small area, try to put it out with the extinguisher. Even if you put the fire out, you should still have the fire department check the site for burning embers. Fires can break out again hours or days later, causing tragedies. Put a fire extinguisher in the tack room, at the end of aisles, and outside the barn in a nearby shed or garage.

- Install lightning rods on your barn. Remember, horses in open fields are at risk for lightning strikes. When the sky is turning black and thunder is rumbling, bring the horses in. Most lightning strikes happen before the rain starts to fall.

- Work out a plan for how you would evacuate the horses. Imagine different scenarios, for example, if the main exit is blocked by burning timbers. Fire experts advise taking out the horse closest to the door first, then getting the others out, if you can do so without endangering your own life.

Do what you can to reduce the risk of fire. Every life is precious.

- Draw a diagram of your barn and house, marking the doors, windows, and all exits. Keep this diagram in the house.
- Current thinking among horse rescue experts is that a blindfold is not always the best method to use when removing panicked horses from a burning building. Many horses are frightened by not being able to see and become even more unmanageable, especially if they have never had a blindfold on before. However, if nothing else is working, try it. Do not wet the cloth because a wet cloth will hold more heat than a dry one.
- Locate a stable where you could take the horses in case of an emergency such as a fire or a destructive storm.

Your support team is invaluable to your horse's well-being and to your peace of mind. Prepare in advance for their visits, be humble, be nice, and pay your bills on time.

6 Performance Events

Attending any type of competition or training seminar is an excellent way to learn more about horses. Watching and interacting with other riders, trainers, and horses allows you to compare methods; perhaps this exposure will inspire you to reach higher levels. The experience will also give you insight into the ups and downs of life with horses— they can surprise you at any time.

When I was sixteen, I worked all summer with my mare Idget to get ready for a show in September. I learned how to braid a mane and tail, and we had lessons and schooled in the ring every other day. We practiced loading and unloading with a friend's trailer. I thought I was prepared for everything.

Finally, the big day came. When we arrived, she came out of the trailer wide-eyed and snorting. I discovered a challenge I had never considered: the chaotic atmosphere of the show grounds.

The roar of the trucks and trailers overwhelmed Idget. She was also faced with people and horses walking everywhere, and the constant crackle and boom of announcements from the loudspeaker. Frightened by the commotion, she trumpeted neighs across the show ring, sounding more like a mad elephant on a charge than a scared mare.

I walked her around to try and settle her down. However, Thoroughbreds have great stamina, and she only got more

Competition
sharpens many
areas of equestrian
skills. Andrew
Philbrick and
Whist.

Far right: Observing
master horsemen
and women at
events can inspire
you to reach higher
levels. Hans
Dressler and Friedel
at the World Eques-
trian Games Selec-
tion Trials at the
USET Olympic
Training Center in
Gladstone, New
Jersey.

nervous. By this point, I was embarrassed and just wanted to
leave, but I did not want to waste the day.

We were entered in an English Pleasure class, which was
anything but pleasurable. At the canter, she escalated to a hand
gallop, and it took several swift rounds of the ring to get her under
control. By the end of the day, I was very relieved when she was
back on the trailer and we were driving home.

Our next show, a month later, was a much better experience.
Well, most of it was. Since nothing bad had happened the last
time, she settled down within a half hour after arrival. In the first
class, she responded well to my aids. I was very pleased until the
command came to canter. Then, after only three strides, the chin-
strap on my helmet broke. The helmet flew off and landed right
on Idget's rump. She bounded forward like a deer. Fortunately, the
ring steward was nimble and was able to get out of our way. No
one was hurt.

Even though things went haywire in the beginning, the shows

and training clinics we attended that year really taught us a lot. My mare and I learned to depend on each other whether we were at home or away.

Before going to an event, the following points may help you and your horse get ready. They may also make it possible to settle in more comfortably while there. Remember to check your tack and equipment before you mount up, especially your helmet.

Preparation for your event

Allow your horse to see and sniff all new tack. Clip has had this saddle on. He looks baffled because he is seeing it in a different location.

TACK. Introduce anything new or different that you plan to use, such as a new bit, bridle, or saddle, a week beforehand. Give him plenty of time to get used to the sight and scent of every item. Horses need to examine things thoroughly before they are convinced new items are harmless.

When your horse is satisfied with the appearance, slowly touch him with the article in a neutral zone like the shoulder area. Praise him when he is brave. Wait until he has lost all suspicion before placing the article on him. This may seem like a slow process, but it only takes a few moments to accomplish. Practice riding him in any new tack. Remember that your leg and hand aids might feel different to him.

SHOW CLOTHES. Let him see, smell, and touch you in your show clothes at home before the event. A horse really notices the scent and appearance of clothes. My mare Sierra is immediately suspicious of anything different I wear. A new jacket or hat is a cause for critical concern. The first time she saw me in a hooded raincoat, she jumped and flew to the back of the stall. She refused to come over until she heard my voice. Even then, she wasn't too sure because I still seemed like a hooded monster to her.

HOOVES. If your horse's feet need trimming or new shoes,

Let your horse check out your new or different attire.

schedule the farrier's visit for at least a week before a show. Allow this much leeway because some horses become slightly lame for a few days after the visit.

VETERINARIAN. For traveling, you'll need a current certificate of health (within thirty days) for your horse and a copy of the Coggins test. Update your inoculations to protect your horse against any diseases he might come in contact with at the event.

CAMERAS. Have plenty of film on hand if someone is available to take photos of you and your horse working. The photos may reveal things you didn't notice about your position. Filming with a video camera offers an ideal way to let you view the brutal truth or happy surprises about your riding. If you are going to a seminar with a trainer, check ahead; some trainers do not allow video cameras.

YOUR FOCUS. Make a list of the main goals you want to accomplish. This can keep you on track and provide a greater sense of achievement. For a seminar, clarifying your goals helps to pinpoint a specific problem area you'd like to work on with the trainer.

INFORMATION TO SHARE WITH YOUR HORSE. Some animal communicators advise preparing a horse for an event by telling him exactly what will be happening there. They suggest explaining where you are going, what day, his traveling companions, what the place will look like, how long he will be there, and when he will return home. Emphasize that you are not moving him again, just traveling, and that you'll be with him. Ask him to help you show other people how well he is doing with his training or work. In effect, enlist his cooperation.

FEEDING. The night before you go, provide a very light meal of grain or give none at all. Bring plenty of hay with you even though multiple-day competitions usually have hay suppliers on site. Bring some of your own so you can mix the new hay in with the old. Many horses feel more comfortable eating from their own feed and water buckets.

The camera can capture the details of your performance.

WATER. Horses will often back off from the taste of unfamiliar water. Dehydration is a serious problem, so take steps to encourage your horse to drink. Many riders flavor their horses' water with molasses, peppermint, or cider vinegar for a few days before, during, and after the event. Only a small amount is needed, about a teaspoon in a full bucket of water.

Transportation issues

When leasing or arranging for a commercial van, make your reservations at least two weeks ahead of time; earlier is better. If your horse hasn't been in a trailer in a while, practice a few loading sessions. Always hitch the trailer to the truck before loading a horse.

If there isn't a trailer you can use on the property, then practice a few refresher lessons in stop and go: halting in hand, then going forward on command. Establishing the willingness to go forward is the whole principle of going into a trailer. Be patient

Practice loading him into the trailer when you have plenty of time.

and try to make it fun. A horse is more responsive when the trainer is patient and cheerful, giving directions clearly.

You'll be glad you took the time to practice loading. It's frustrating to be packed and ready and then have the horse refuse to go into the trailer. It's also just as exasperating at the other end of the day, when you are exhausted and hungry, standing in front of

The excitement of competition flows between you and your horse.

the trailer, and your horse won't budge. Tempers flare on such occasions, and the frustration can result in cruel and harsh solutions. If your horse does resist loading, invest in a professional trainer to work with him.

Many trainers will load an older mare or gelding first to show a young horse that there is nothing to worry about. It's natural for a horse to trust another horse's judgment. This is the system police departments rely on when training horse recruits. They pair the new horses with the older, unflappable veterans of the streets. The new horse will soon imitate the other one's calm behavior.

For the same reason, trainers will bring young horses with experienced ones to show grounds or racetracks. This helps the young horses to relax, become used to the commotion, and build their confidence before they are expected to perform or compete.

Traveling day

When you are going somewhere and have a big day planned, you can't help being a little excited. Your horse will be, too. He will know something is up the minute you step in the barn, especially if his regular routine is different. As mentioned above, it's best to omit the grain. If you must feed him, do so at least two hours before leaving.

While getting him ready for transport, remember to check his hooves for stones before putting his shipping boots or bandages on. When the trailer pulls up, he may become harder to handle. Breathing deeply and using soft words can help ease his nervousness somewhat.

When you are traveling to a one-day event, leave as early as possible. You need to allow your horse enough time to recover his physical strength and emotional composure after you arrive. In case you get lost while driving, you will be glad for the extra time. I know the wisdom of this piece of advice because I am an expert at getting lost.

If the distance to the event amounts to four or more hours in the trailer, consider arriving the day before. For a journey lasting

eight to ten hours, arriving at the site two days prior to the event reduces the risk of contracting illnesses such as shipping fever.

Research into transport-related stress suggests that horses should not travel more than eight hours or four hundred miles without stopping for rest. After this point, the incidence of stress-related illnesses and infections rises dramatically. The total time on the trailer during any one day should not exceed twelve hours.

Horses being shipped distances over twelve hours should only be worked at a walk for five days after arrival. This is a precaution to prevent episodes of tying–up, a painful disorder. Performance horses competing in events that require great exertion, such as racing and jumping, are advised to arrive at the site a week to two weeks before to recover the maximum ability to perform.

Horses are susceptible to heat exhaustion and dehydration while riding in trailers, so avoid traveling during the hottest part of the day. These conditions need to be taken very seriously. If ignored and untreated, they can lead to cardiac arrhythmia, collapse, convulsions, and even death.

Early signs of dehydration

■ Eyes become dull and may appear sunken.

■ Capillary refill is slow. To check, press a spot on the gums; it will appear white. Release the pressure. If the area takes more than two seconds to return to a red color, that's a slow response.

■ Pinch test. In front of the shoulder, pinch a fold of skin. A fold that stays in place for more than two seconds is a sign of dehydration.

SOLUTIONS. Immediately provide the horse with water. You could also give some water that has been mixed with electrolytes, but only if the horse is used to the taste. Otherwise, the unfamiliar scent of the electrolytes might cause him to refuse the water.

DANGER SIGNS. If your horse shows any of these signs, seek veterinary help immediately.

■ No interest in food or drink.

■ Disoriented and acting confused.

■ Dry gums and nostrils.

■ Muscle spasms.

■ Scant amount of urine.

Early signs of hyperthermia

Hyperthermia is heat exhaustion. Consult your vet if any of these signs appear.

■ Temperature over 103 degrees F.

■ Shallow and rapid respiration rate of over fifty breaths per minute.

■ Heart rate over eighty beats a minute.

■ Extreme sweating all over the body.

■ Gut sounds that diminish or disappear.

■ Restless and irritable behavior.

■ Bright red gums.

SOLUTIONS. Sponge the horse off with cold water, concentrating on the head, neck, and legs. Take the horse to an area where there is shade and a breeze. Let the horse graze because the water content in the grass can help replenish fluids. If no grass is available, wet down his hay.

DANGER SIGNS. Seek veterinary help at once for any of these signs:

- Sweating stops and the skin feels dry and hot to the touch.
- Rapid breathing continues or gets faster and even shallower.
- Disoriented behavior.
- Dark red gums. This is a serious sign that the horse's circulatory system is being overwhelmed.
- Thumps or synchronous diaphragmatic flutter. This is a condition resulting from fluid loss due to excessive sweating. The belly muscles may shake with a quick, abrupt motion like hiccups.
- Temperature continues to rise. At 107 to 108 degrees F., the organs will start to fail, producing convulsions, coma, and eventually death.
- Collapse. The muscles will tremble while he is lying on the ground. He may struggle violently to get up.

Even though this information addresses some equine health problems, it's a good idea to take a veterinary reference book with you when you travel with your horse. Use the reference book to look up any symptoms you are concerned about and to determine what to do. Usually, a reference book will also include basic first aid and instructions for bandaging minor wounds.

Arrival at the event

At last, you're at the site, and it is a busy scene. Remind yourself that taking your horse off the trailer in a slow and calm manner is as important as being patient while loading. Injuries during unloading are all too common.

Remember not to unhitch your trailer from the truck while your horse is still inside. If two horses are on the trailer, keep the first one off the trailer nearby until the second one is unloaded. Otherwise, the horse still inside may panic, thinking he is being left behind.

Never underestimate the power and danger of a frightened horse. Panicked horses can cause extreme damage to their handlers, themselves, and the trailers. Never get in a trailer with a panicked horse. Bring another horse near the trailer so the scared horse can see it; that should help calm him down.

The first reaction many people have when a horse is acting up is to yell, "Whoa!" However, that is not helpful because shouting only scares a horse more. A quiet hushing sound and speaking his name softly will work better as a distraction.

Settling in at the site

A WALK ABOUT. Once your horse is off the trailer, walk him around for ten to twenty minutes to stretch his legs and become familiar with the grounds. Due to the risk of infection and unpredictable behavior, do not let your horse touch noses or share buckets with strange horses. What looks like a friendly sniff could quickly erupt into a painful nip or strike.

It's fun to see all the well-dressed riders and horses at the show.

HORSE WATCH. Once the walk is over, you can tie your horse to the trailer or a sturdy tree, but fence boards are not safe or strong

enough. In addition, do not leave a horse alone. Someone should always watch over the horse. If a horse breaks free and gallops about, he's a danger to himself and everyone else. Portable corrals are useful to safely enclose a horse. Never leave the horse on the trailer. The temperature climbs rapidly in an enclosed place like that, sometimes as much as twenty degrees in a few minutes.

RISK OF INFECTION. Any place where a lot of horses are in close proximity presents the possibility of exposure to illness or disease. Avoid grazing your horse in well-worn areas since there is a greater risk of coming in contact with parasites and worm eggs. Because some viruses are airborne, be on the alert for any horse that is repeatedly coughing or that has a nasal discharge. It's better to leave the site and forfeit an entry fee than to have your horse become ill and infect the horses at home.

FEEDING.   The horse's gut functions will be stressed by the transport and the excitement of the day. Play it safe and avoid giving any grain. If you must, give just a token handful while at the event. If you are at a multi-day competition or seminar and your horse needs the extra nutrition, cut the grain ration in half and give extra hay. After any meal of grain, allow one to two hours of rest before working the horse.

HAY.   Chewing on hay helps horses breathe deeper, and it promotes calmness. Hay also keeps water in the gut, lessening the risk of impaction colic.

SPECTATORS.   Watch out for spectators who may wander up to your horse. Many people have no idea how to act or to behave around a horse, nor do they have any idea how dangerous a kick or bite can be. Some parents will even let small children come up and walk around a horse's legs. Protect the children and your horse by asking people to keep a safe distance.

THE WARM-UP RING.   This is a busy place with horses and riders jogging, trotting, cantering, loping, longeing and jumping in all

Hugo Huesca and Lancelot in the warm-up ring.

different areas and directions of the ring. It can be quite overwhelming to a horse that has never been to an event. Keep to the rail until your horse gets used to the scene.

Safeguard your horse by keeping at least a full horse's length between you and the horse ahead. Double that length if a horse has a red ribbon tied to his tail, indicating that he is a kicker. Stay alert for horses that pin their ears flat back when you are passing. This is an aggressive threat. Dominant horses will savage another horse, biting him on the neck if the opportunity arises.

If you take practice jumps, pick up any poles that your horse might knock down. Finally, take it easy while warming up since your horse will need a reserve of energy to put on his best performance.

A MULTI-DAY EVENT. Permanent stabling is available at many of the large show locations. Before you turn your horse into the

stall, check it over to make sure it is clean. Look carefully for any sharp edges or nails protruding from the walls.

Your hard work and polish will pay off.

Establish a routine right away. In caring for your horse, do the same things at the same time each day, such as feeding him at seven and taking him out at eight. A set routine and some extra affection will help your horse feel more secure.

Calming your performance anxiety

Quieting your own nervousness can be difficult. All your hard work comes down to this brief precious time in the spotlight, and no one wants to be embarrassed in front of other riders, friends, and relatives. Riders in various disciplines resort to similar strategies to reduce tension, and you might find the following helpful:

- Deep breathing exercises can ease your mind and relax tense muscles.
- Avoid coffee or cola to eliminate the jagged feelings provoked by caffeine. Cut back on high-sugar snacks and choose protein foods such as peanut butter.
- Maintain a positive attitude. Keep winning and losing in perspective. If you win, great. If you don't, there's always next

Relax into your best performance. Reining champions Bryant Pace and Gunner.

time. Remember that good sportsmanship will put you and your horse in the best light in front of the judge. Criticizing other riders in public will come back to haunt you, and voicing complaints about the judge's decision is equally undesirable.

■ Practice visualization techniques. Plan your ride in detail in your mind's eye, visualizing exactly how you want your ride to look. This is a method that has been utilized by people in many

Maximize your potential for success in competition by having your horse properly conditioned. Norma C. House and Eowyn Elan Song at the USET Endurance Championship at the USET Olympic Training Center, Gladstone, New Jersey.

Eventing is one of many exciting and varied sports you can enjoy with your horse. Momi K. Black riding Chort.

sports. Performance improves during the actual riding when your mind is free because you know what you're going to do.

Exercises of progressive relaxation, in which you imagine relaxing your whole body from head to toe, can be useful while warming up before your event. They are also helpful before schooling horses at home. These exercises establish the habit of being calm and quiet before riding. When you relax, you feel safer.

Once this habit is associated with daily riding, it will carry over to the performance ring. The horse will be more nervous when away from home, but the established relaxation routine will help to calm him down. Of course, avoid these exercises if your horse is going into an event where speed is important.

Attending a show or seminar could be just the stimulus you and your horse need to move on to the next level of training. Just weathering the experience together can make your relationship stronger, and it will certainly show you all the equestrian skills you still need to master!

7 Finding a New Home

Life is constantly changing. Things might be going smoothly at your horse's stable for a while. Suddenly, something occurs that makes it necessary for you to find new accommodations.

Ideally, you'll have notice ahead of time. However, sometimes you'll have little if any notice. For example, if an owner experiences financial setbacks, he might have to close his stable immediately. On the other hand, a change might be your idea. You may feel that another stable offers more challenging opportunities to ride and learn, or it would be a more comfortable environment for your horse.

Here are the basic requirements you want for a new equine home:

- Gentle caregivers who respect the horses and the stable help.
- Roomy hazard-free box stalls that are at least twelve feet by twelve feet.
- Good-quality hay and the freedom to feed your own type of grain.
- Availability of daily turnout.
- Large pasture that is not too crowded and that has safe fencing and gates.
- Riding ring to train in and trails nearby.

Keep your horse's well-being and happiness uppermost in your mind when choosing another stable or selecting a new owner.

Facing page:
Above: An attractive stable shows organization and attention to detail.

Below: Roomy stalls are very desirable. This one looks more comfortable than my first apartment.

Once when I was faced with a stabling predicament, I visited several farms in the immediate area. Location was very important because I would be driving back and forth every day. Another factor was the number and size of the horses my mare would be living with. Sierra is only 13.2 hands. I didn't want her to be intimidated by having to fight for her food amidst huge horses.

After searching for three days, I was starting to feel desperate because I only had six days to move Sierra. Fortunately, a friend came to my rescue and put me in touch with a veterinarian who

had a boarding stable nearby. The facility included a separate paddock and a run-in shed where Sierra could spend her quarantine period. Four other mares and a gelding lived there. It was a diverse group consisting of a Thoroughbred, an Appaloosa, a Quarter Horse, an Arabian, and a young Connemara gelding.

When moving day came, my friend brought her trailer over to transport Sierra. Walking away from the stable, Sierra acted unsettled and suspicious. She planted her feet in front of the trailer. She didn't intend on going anywhere. We talked to her for a few minutes, telling her that she would be fine in her new home. She didn't budge.

I walked her in a circle, bringing her in front of the trailer. She stopped again. I told her that there were other horses there and lots of pear trees (she loves pears). She looked back at the fields, trees, and barn that she'd come to know as home, took a deep breath, sighed, and walked into the trailer.

Arriving at the new farm, Sierra was scared, excited, and extremely interested in the other horses. The separate paddock

Far left: The quality of the pastures is an important consideration.

The availability of riding trails and schooling facilities are crucial factors, too.

Sierra frequently relocated to new stables during our first year together. This is her "Where am I going now?" expression.

was ideal. She could see and hear everyone, and she could learn the pecking order by watching from afar instead of being pecked on. She also enjoyed munching on many a pear.

Two weeks later when she joined the herd, a few rounds of chasing and a few nips established her in fifth place behind the mares. Once she discovered that the gelding liked to play, they had a great time rearing up and playing wild horses.

Sierra was very content there. However, nine months later, destiny dealt her a new card when my family and I were able to buy a small farm with a horse barn. Since horses should never be kept alone, the owner of the Arabian mare graciously allowed us to bring her to our place to keep Sierra company until we found another horse.

On moving day, the Arabian mare, Zeke, calmly walked in the trailer as if she were going into a stall to eat dinner. This gave Sierra confidence, and she walked right in, too. After their arrival, Sierra was nervous, but she was soon having fun exploring the yard, the pasture, and her new stall.

Over the next two weeks, we let the mares out in the pasture for a short time each afternoon. We started with a half hour and increased the time by fifteen minutes every day, so their digestive systems could get adjusted to the new grass.

Zeke lived with us until her owner bought a farm, and so she moved over there. We then adopted Battle Clip from the Standardbred Retirement Foundation in New Jersey, and Sierra's new herd consisted of a gelding and a mare.

Selling your horse

Horses rarely spend their entire lifetime with one owner. People move up to higher levels of competition or change disciplines, and young people outgrow ponies and small horses. If you must sell your horse, here are some ways to attract sincere buyers and to discourage unwanted inquiries from those who deal in the slaughter trade.

A horse this handsome and well-groomed would attract many buyers.

ADVERTISEMENTS. To catch the eye of potential buyers, list the horse's most outstanding feature or quality, such as special training, appearance or personality, first in the ad. Most ads will list breed type, size, age, color, experience and/or accomplishments, the asking price, a contact person, phone number, e-mail, and website address. Some websites will contain video clips that show the horse at home or in competition.

This sample ad contains the type of information generally used:

> Nimble Nell. Flashy hunter/jumper prospect. 16.1 H, 6 y.o. chestnut mare with white socks. Well-mannered, great with children, bombproof on trails, started over fences. Owner leaving for college. Asking $6,500 or best offer. Contact Nancy at 555-1212. E-mail at horseforsale@site.net or see a video clip of Nell on our website at www.nimblenell.com.

The horse's name is sometimes given to make the horse more personable and appealing. A name like Majestic Delight sounds good, but if the horse's name is Trouble, leave it out!

Some ads hint at the reason for the sale with short explanations like, "sadly outgrown" or "no time." This is useful information because many people like to know why a horse being portrayed as so wonderful is being offered for sale.

Highlight your horse's good points in the ad but don't exaggerate. For example, be honest about his level of training. The new owner may become so disenchanted when the horse doesn't live up to the glowing praise that he turns around and resells him.

Common abbreviations used in advertisements include:

- ■ H or hh = hands high
- ■ 7 y.o. = 7 years old
- ■ OBO = or best offer
- ■ 5K = $5,000
- ■ Neg. = negotiable price
- ■ PC/4H prospect = a safe mount for the Pony Club or the 4-H program

- H/J = hunter/ jumper
- TB = Thoroughbred
- QH = Quarter Horse or AQHA (registered with American Quarter Horse Association)
- DWB = Dutch Warmblood
- WB/X = warmblood cross or a warmblood mixed with another breed
- LFG = live foal guaranteed (used in stallion ads)
- "Lots of chrome" = flashy white markings
- "A" Circuit = horse has been shown at high levels of competition
- "Bombproof" = steady to ride and can handle stressful situations

For a photo ad, make sure the photo is clear and focused. Take it on a bright day with an uncluttered background. The horse should be well-groomed and have on an attractive halter or tack. The handler, if shown, should be in plain, dark clothes. If the horse is pictured under saddle, the rider should wear the correct clothes for the discipline for which the horse is being advertised.

When advertising in equine newspapers and magazines and on websites, don't use the term, "free to good home." Killer buyers will look for such wording. They will entertain no guilt about making a quick profit from your generosity by taking your horse to the slaughter yard.

AUCTION PRECAUTIONS. Selling your horse at an auction should be a last resort. Sale yards are stressful, traumatic places. Unfortunately, many horses are sold as meat on the hoof at auctions.

MEDICAL CONSIDERATIONS. Make sure your horse's health records are current and update them if necessary. These records are valuable to prospective buyers. They can learn about your horse's health history and what ongoing care will be needed. In addition, they also give the schedule for worming and farrier care.

A GOOD MATCH. Try and ensure that your horse will have a suitable owner when he leaves your care. Determine whether the person looking at your horse would be a good match for him. Are the buyer's riding style and goals consistent with what your horse can actually do or does he at least have the potential? If the buyer's plans include showing or long trail rides, does your horse enjoy these things without getting overly stressed?

ALTERNATIVES TO SELLING. You may also consider the possibility of donating your horse if he is sound and emotionally stable. Several different types of programs will accept donations of horses. These include therapeutic riding establishments, mounted police units, and college equestrian teams.

Some programs have criteria such as to age, training level, or temperament. For example, horses used by the police have age and size limitations. On the other hand, therapeutic riding programs feel that older horses are more desirable because they tend to be calmer and less apt to act out.

Occasionally, horses are donated as companion horses to keep solo horses company or as "babysitters" to set a good example of behavior with groups of weanlings or yearlings. Some horses have even found useful new occupations as shepherds, herding and guarding flocks of sheep from prowling coyotes. Horses are certainly versatile workers and friends.

Saying goodbye

We have long understood that horses in transition are mentally and physically fragile, but we now know that the transition period

Goodbyes are never easy.

when horses are vulnerable extends through the first week and even longer. The most important concepts to keep in mind include taking precautions during transport, being careful what you feed your horse, and giving him plenty of quiet and relaxation time after he arrives. And all should go smoothly.

I'm a firm believer in the reality that horses understand what we say and feel. I think it is only fair to talk to your horse about what is ahead for him, whether you believe he will understand or not. He should be mentally prepared for his new life. It's a worthwhile effort to try to prevent the trauma that comes with a sudden departure. Unfortunately, horses are often simply loaded up and taken away from everything near and dear to them: friends, food, and their favorite places to scratch, graze, and gallop.

Far right: May you experience the joy of a horse's devotion.

Farewell!

Be considerate and tell your horse about any upcoming changes. Let him know when he is relocating to a different farm or going to another owner. This way he can go forward with courage to his new stable, settle in safely, and make himself at home again.

Bibliography

1 Before the Van Arrives

Barakat, Christine. "Road Tests: How Shipping Affects Horses." *Equus*, April 2000.

Bonner, Laurie. "Safe on Arrival." *Equus*, August 2001.

Guay, Mary, and Donna Schlinkert. *Buying Your First Horse*. Marietta, GA: White Papers Press, 1997.

Hayes, Karen. *Hands-On Horse Care*. North Pomfret, VT: Trafalgar Square Publishing, 1997.

Hill, Cherry. *Horse Health Care*. Pownal, VT: Storey Communications, 1994.

2 Moving into a New Home

Blake, Henry. *Talking with Horses*. New York: E.P. Dutton, 1976.

Cregier, Sharon. "Crusader for Equine Rights," *American Horseman*, February 1975.

Dorrance, Tom. *True Unity*. Tuscarora, NV: Give-It-A-Go Enterprises, 1987.

Haworth, Josephine. *The Horsemasters: The Secret of Understanding Horses*. London: Methuen, 1983.

Podhajsky, Alois. *My Horses, My Teachers*. New York: Doubleday, 1968.

Pony Boy, GaWaNi. *Horse, Follow Closely*. Irvine, CA: Bow Tie Press, 1998.

Rarey, John S. *The Modern Art of Taming Wild Horses*. Columbus, OH: Ohio State Journal Company, 1855.

Roberts, Tom. *Horse Control — The Young Horse*. Richmond, South Australia: T.A. and P.R. Roberts, 1974.

Williams, Moyra. *Horse Psychology*. Reprint. London: J.A. Allen & Co., 1986.

Woodhouse, Barbara. *Talking to Animals*. New York: Berkeley Books, 1983.

3 Keeping Peace in the Pasture

Budiansky, Stephen. *The World According to Horses*. New York: Henry Holt, 2000.

Crabbe, Barbara. "Is Your Horse's Fencing Safe?" *Horse & Rider*, May 2002.

Eustis-Cross, Barbara, and Nancy Bowker. *The Wild Horse: An Adopter's Manual*. New York: Howell Book House, 1992.

Marie, Trish. "Seven Solutions for Troubled Herds." *Equus*, October 1998.

Roberts, Monty. *Shy Boy: The Horse That Came In from the Wild*. New York: HarperCollins, 2000.

Ryden, Hope. *America's Last Wild Horses*. New York: E.P. Dutton, 1970.

_____. *Wild Horses I Have Known*. New York: Clarion Books, 1999.

Vavra, Robert. *Equus: The Creation of a Horse*. New York: William Morrow, 1977.

4 Stress Reducers for Horses

Boone, J. Allen. *Kinship with All Life*. New York: Harper & Row, 1954.

Brennan, Mary. *The Complete Holistic Care and Healing for Horses*. North Pomfret, VT: Trafalgar Square Publishing, 2001.

Curtis, Anita. *Animal Wisdom: Communications with Animals*. Gilbertsville, PA: Anita Curtis, 1996.

Gaynor, Mitchell. *The Sounds of Healing*. New York: Broadway Books, 1999.

Gray, Peter. *The Organic Horse*. Newton Abbot, England: David & Charles, 2000.

Holderness-Roddam, Jane. *The Horse Companion*. Hauppauge, NY: Barron's, 1997.

Kohanov, Linda. *The Tao of Equus*. Novato, CA: New World Library, 2001.

McFarland, Cynthia. "Acupuncture, Chiropractic, and Massage Therapy." *Northeast Equine Journal*, January 1999.

Meagher, Jack. *Beating Muscle Injuries for Horses*. Rowley, MA: Hamilton Horse Associates, 1985.

Roades, Michael J. *Talking with Nature*. Tiburon, CA: H.J. Kramer, Inc., 1987.

Smith, Penelope. *When Animals Speak*. Point Reyes, CA: Pegasus Publications, 1993.

Summer Rain, Mary. *Spirit Song*. Charlottesville, VA: Hampton Roads Publishing, 1985.

Tellington-Jones, Linda, and Ursula Bruns. *The Tellington-Jones Equine Awareness Method*. Millwood, NY: Breakthrough Publications, 1988.

Zidonis, Nancy A., and Marie K. Soderberg. *Equine Acupressure: A Treatment Workbook*. Parker, CO: Equine Acupressure Inc., 1991.

5 Your Support Team

Gager, Ed, and Bob Rhodes. *Sound Mouth, Sound Horse*. Vincentown, NJ: Emerson Publishing, 1983.

Hayes, Horace. *Veterinary Notes for Horse Owners*. rev. ed. London: Stanley Paul Ltd., 1964.

King, Marcia. "Open Wide—Equine Dental Care." *Horse Illustrated*, July 2002.

Mettler, John. *Horse Sense*. Pownal, VT: Storey Communications, 1989.

Seegal, Jane. "The Worst That Can Happen—Barn Fires." *Equus*, Feb. 2001.

Smith, Carin A. *Easy Health Care for Your Horse*. New York: Prentice Hall Press, 1991.

Sweat, Rebecca. "You and Your Veterinarian." *Western Horseman*, April 1998.

6 Performance Events

Haas, Jessie. *Safe Horse, Safe Rider*. Pownal, VT: Storey Communications, 1994.

Hill, Cherry. *From the Center of the Ring*. Pownal, VT: Storey Communications, 1988.

Savoie, Jane. *That Winning Feeling!* North Pomfret, VT: Trafalgar Square Publishing, 1992.

Stoneridge, M.A. *A Horse of Your Own*. New York: Doubleday, 1968.

Swift, Sally. *Centered Riding*. North Pomfret, VT: Trafalgar Square Publishing, 1985.

Henderson, Carolyn. *The Horse Owner's Survival Guide*. Shrewsbury, England: Swan Hill Press, 1998.

Jacobsen, Patricia, and Marcia Hayes. *A Horse Around the House*. New York: Crown Publishers, 1972.

McDonald, Mary Ashby. *Starting and Running Your Own Horse Business*. Pownal, VT: Storey Communications, 1997.

Wanless, Mary. *For the Good of the Horse*. North Pomfret, VT: Trafalgar Square Publishing, 1997.

Appendix:

Resources for Information and Associations

Adoption and Rescue Organizations

ASPCA National Headquarters
American Society for the Prevention of Cruelty to Animals
424 East 92nd Street
New York, NY 10128-6804
(212) 876-7700
www.aspca.org

The Brooke Hospital for Animals
Broadmead House
21 Panton Street
London, SW1Y 4DR England
020 7930 0210
www.brooke-hospital.org.uk
Rescue work for horses, donkeys, and mules in Egypt, Pakistan, Jordan, and India.

Brumby Watch Australia Inc.
MS 194 Range View Drive
Gatton, Queensland, 4343 Australia
07 54622 337
www.brumbywatchaustralia.com

Department of the Interior
Bureau of Land Management
Wild Horse and Burro Program
1849 C Street, N.W., Mail Stop

406-LS
Washington, D.C. 20240-0001
1-866-4 MUSTANGS
www.wildhorseandburro.blm.gov or
www.adoptahorse.blm.gov for
Internet adoptions.

Equine Advocates and Rescue
Services, Inc.
P.O. Box 123
Buninyong, Victoria 3357
Australia
0407 412 327
e-mail: *earspresident@yahoo.com.au*

Equine Rescue League
P.O. Box 4366
Leesburg, VA 20177
(703) 771-1240
www.equinerescueleague.org

Foal Trek
3539 St-Charles, Box 398
Kirkland, Quebec H9H 3C4 Canada
(514) 916-1254
www.foaltrek.com
PMU foal placement in Canada and the U.S.

Habitat for Horses
P.O. Box 213
Hitchcock, TX 77563
(409) 935-0277
www.habitatforhorses.org

Heaven Can Wait Equine Rescue
R.R. #1
Cameron, Ontario   KOM 1GO
Canada
(705) 359-3766
www.heavencanwaitequinerescue.org

Hooved Animal Humane Society
P.O. Box 400
Woodstock, IL 60098
(815) 337-5563
www.hahs.org

Mustang and Burro Organized
Assistance
P.O. Box 601
Barrington, NH 03825
(603) 664-2787

ReRun Recycling Racehorses
P.O. Box 96
Carlisle, KY 40311
(859) 289-7786
www.rerun.org

RSPCA
Royal Society for the Prevention of
Cruelty to Animals
Wilberforce Way, Southwater
Horsham, West Sussex RH13 9RS
England
0870 3335 999
www.rspca.org.uk

Standardbred Retirement
Foundation
P.O. Box 763, 49 East Main Street
Freehold, NJ 07728
(732) 462-8773
www.adoptahorse.org

Trallwm Farm
Carmarthen, Wales UK
08707 469232
www.trallwmfarm.co.uk
A sanctuary for horses and animals
at risk.

Animal Communication and Equine Therapy Programs (a selection)

Canadian Therapeutic Riding
Association
e-mail: *ctra@golden.net*
Ciancio Animal Communications
e-mail: *cciancio@animail.net*

Anita Curtis
Animal Communications
P.O. Box 182
Gilbertsville, PA 19525

(610) 327-3820
www.anitacurtis.com

Linda Kohanov
Epona Equestrian Services
4551 North Araibi Place
Tucson, AZ 85749
(520) 760-0003
www.taoofequus.com

N.A.R.H.A.
North American Riding for the
Handicapped Association
P.O. Box 33150
Denver, CO 80233
(800) 369-7433
www.narha.org
This site also has listings for
programs in Canada.

Riding for the Disabled
Association of England
Lavinia Norfolk House
Avenue R
Stoneleigh Park, Warwickshire
CV8 2LY England
024 7669 6510
www.riding-for-disabled.org.uk

Riding for the Disabled
Association of Australia
P.O. Box 424
Ascot Vale, Victoria 3032
Australia
03 9372 2126
www.rda.org.au

Penelope Smith
Animal Communication Specialist
Anima Mundi Incorporated
P.O. Box 1060
Point Reyes, CA 94956
(415) 663-1247
www.animaltalk.net
Extensive list of animal communi-
cators in the U.S. and Europe.

Health Care

American Association of Equine
Practitioners
4075 Iron Works Parkway,
Building D
Lexington, KY 40511
(859) 233-0147
www.aaep.org

American Holistic Veterinary
Medical Association
2218 Old Emmorton Road
Bel Air, MD 21015
(410) 569-0795
e-mail: *ahvma@compuserve.com*

Equine Centre, University of
Melbourne
250 Princes Highway

Werribee, Victoria 3030 Australia
03 9731 2304
www.equinecentre.com.au
Practical horse care and medical
information.

Helios Homeopathic Pharmacy
97 Camden Road
Tunbridge Wells, Kent TN1 2QR
England
01892 536393
www.helios.co.uk

Lyn Kamer
The Healing Touch of New Jersey
Equine Sports Massage Therapy
(856) 740-2869

Nelson Bach USA, Ltd.
100 Research Drive
Wilmington, MA 01887-4406
(800) 314-BACH
www.nelsonbach.com
Supplier of Bach flower essences.
The web-site links to offices in the
U.K. and Canada.

NetVet
www.netvet.wustl.edu/horses.htm
Internet horse health information.

SP Equine Health and Herbal
38/40 Broton Estate
Halstead, Essex CO9 1HB
England
01787 476400
www.equinehealthandherbal.co.uk

Magazines

Canadian Horseman
Horse Publications Group
225 Industrial Parkway, S.
P.O. Box 670
Aurora, Ontario L4G 4J9
Canada
(416) 727-0107
www.horse-canada.com

The Chronicle of the Horse
P.O. Box 46
Middleburg, VA 20118
(540) 687-6341
www.chronofhorse.com

Equus
656 Quince Orchard Road,
Suite 600
Gaithersburg, MD 20878
(301) 977-3900
www.equusmagazine.com

Horse Illustrated
P.O. Box 6050
Mission Viejo, CA 92690
(949) 855-8822
www.animalnetwork.com

The Horse Magazine
P.O. Box 349
Pakenham, Victoria 3810
Australia
03 5942 7447
www.horsemagazine.com

Horse & Rider
P.O. Box 4101
Golden, CO 80401
(303) 278-1010
www.horseandrider.com

Horse & Rider (UK)
D.J. Murphy Publishers Ltd.
Haslemere House
Lower Street, Haslemere
Surrey GU27 2PE England
01428 651551
www.horseandridermagazine.co.uk

Western Horseman
P.O. Box 7980
3850 N. Nevada Avenue
Colorado Springs, CO 80933-7980
(719) 633-5524
www.westernhorseman.com

National and International Organizations

American Horse Council
1700 K Street N.W., Suite 300
Washington, D.C. 20006
(202) 296-4031
www.horsecouncil.org
Legislative representative of the
horse industry.

American Horse Protection
Association
1000 29th Street, N.W., Suite T-100
Washington, D.C.   20007
(202) 965-0500
www.ahpa.us

Australian Horse Industry Council
400 Epsom Road
Flemington, Victoria 3031
Australia
03 9258 4374
www.horsecouncil.org.au

British Horse Society
Stoneleigh Deer Park, Kenilworth
Warwickshire CV8 2XZ England
08701 202244
www.bhs.org.uk

Canadian Federation of Humane
Societies
102-30 Concourse Gate
Nepean, Ontario   K2E 7V7
(613) 224-8072
www.cfhs.ca
National organization dedicated to
improving animals' lives across
Canada.

Humane Society of the United States
2100 L Street, N.W.
Washington, D.C. 20037

(202) 452-1100
www.hsus.org

International League for the
Protection of Horses
Anne Colvin House
Snetterton
Norfolk NR16 2LR   England
0870 870 1927
www.ilph.org

International Society for the
Protection of Mustangs and Burros
P.O. Box 55
Lantry, South Dakota 57636
(605) 964-6866
www.ispmb.com

Irish Horse Board
Block B, Maynooth Business
Campus
Maynooth, Co. Kildare Ireland
1 5053584
www.irishhorseboard.com

Kentucky Horse Park
4089 Iron Works Parkway
Lexington, KY 40511
(800) 678-8813
www.kyhorsepark.com
Educational programs, world class
events, the Hall of Champions,
and changing exhibits at the International Museum of the Horse.

U.S.A. Equestrian Federation
4047 Iron Works Parkway
Lexington, KY 40511-8483
(859) 258-2472
www.equestrian.org

Australian Equine Behaviour
Centre
Clonbinane Road, Broadford,
Victoria   3658   Australia
03 5787 1374
www.aebc.com.au

Greg Barrington
Motivation Training
West Wind Farms
Burnt River, Ontario, Canada
(705) 454-1459
www.gregbarrington.com

Steve Brady
Progressive Horsemanship
124 Germany Lane
Dyers Crossing, NSW   2429
Australia
02 6550 2229
*www.stevebradyhorsemanship.
homestead.com*

Chris Brisbane
Natural Horsemanship
Rushbury, Shropshire, England
07973 84902
www.horsewhispering.co.uk

Kenny Harlow
Cedar Run Ranch
R.R. 3, Box 146
Cumberland, VA 23040
(434) 983-2221
www.kennyharlow.com

John Lyons Symposiums, Inc.
P.O. Box 479
Parachute, CO 81635
(970) 285-9797
www.johnlyons.com

Pat Parelli Natural
Horse.Man.Ship Center
P.O. Box 5950
Pagosa Springs, CO 81147
(800) 642-3335
www.parelli.com

GaWaNi Pony Boy
(570) 325-2012
www.ponyboy.com

Monty Roberts
Flag is Up Farm
P.O. Box 86
Solvang, CA 93464
(888) 826-6689
www.montyroberts.com

TTEAM
Linda Tellington-Jones
P.O. Box 3793
Santa Fe, NM 87506
(800) 854-8326
www.tteam-ttouch.com

Acclaim Tack & Horse Supply
Edmonton, Alberta, Canada
www.acclaimtack.com

Back in the Saddle
570 Turner Drive, Suite D
Durango, CO 81303
(800) 865-2478
www.backinthesaddle.com

Chamisa Ridge, Inc.
P.O. Box 23294
Santa Fe, NM 87502
(800) 743-3188
www.chamisaridge.com
Supplier of herbal and natural
healing products.

Dover Saddlery
P.O. Box 5837
Holliston, MA 01746
(800) 989-1500
www.doversaddlery.com

Hartog's Equestrian Education
Services
P.O. Box 5097
Daisy Hill, Queensland 4127
Australia
+61 7 3209 1648
www.heees.com or
www.horseridingcoach.com
Offers equestrian training products
and a correspondence course.

High Spring Trading Post
General Delivery, R.R. 2
Marmora, Ontario K0K 2M0 Canada
(705) 778-3760
www.highspringtradingpost.com

Horseware Ireland
Dublin Road
Dundalk
Co. Louth, Ireland
42 9389000
www.horseware.com

Ride-Away Saddlery and Country
Clothing
Stillington Road
Sutton-on-the-Forest
York, YO61 1EH England
01347 810443
www.rideaway.co.uk

State Line Tack, Inc.
Route 121, P.O. Box 428
Plaistow, NH 03865
(800) 228-9208
www.statelinetack.com

Tack in the Box
P.O. Box 158
Sublimity, OR 97385
(800) 456-8225
www.tackinthebox.com

TDS Saddlers Ltd.
Lymington Bottom Road
Four Marks, Hampshire GU34
5EW England
01420 562758
www.tds-saddlers.com

Valley Vet Supply
1118 Pony Express Highway
P.O. Box 504
Marysville, KS 66508-0504
(800) 356-1005
www.valleyvet.com

Zilco International Pty Ltd.
P.O. Box 126
Concord West, NSW 2138
Australia
028765 9999
www.zilco.com.au

Harness and saddlery, with satellite offices in England and New Zealand.

Transporation

Alex Nichols Agency
P.O. Box 698
31 Plainfield Avenue
Elmont, NY 11003
(516) 488-8080
www.alexnicholsagency.com
Shipping of horses and livestock worldwide.

All-State Horse Express
(800) 451-7696
www.horse-express.com
Informative web site.

Brook Ledge Horse Transportation
P.O. Box 56
Oley, PA 19547
(800) 523-8143

Equine Express, N.A. Inc.
P.O. Box 501
Pilot Point, TX 76258
(800) 545-9098
www.equineexpress.com

Equine World Internet site
www.equine-world.co.uk
A directory that has links to horse transport services in England.

Global Horse Transport
P.O. Box 358
Lindenhurst, NY 11757
(631) 226-7676
www.globalhorsetransport.com
Domestic and international arrangements.

National Horse Carriers
Association
www.nationalhorsecarriers.com
An organization for transport professionals whose site offers information on transporting horses.

Quarantine station information
All-D-Reiterhof Farm
33 Naughright Road
Long Valley, NJ 07853
(908) 876-1843
www.cemequinequarantine.com

Web-sites and General Horse Directories

www.aushorseresources.net
Australian equestrian sites.

The Canadian Horse site
www.geocities.com/newfie007.geo
With an Equines in Canada Web
ring and useful links pages.

www.canadianhorsetrader.com
Wide-ranging access to equestrian
services in Canada.

www.cybersteed.com
Equine nutrition and medical
information.

www.equerry.com
Helpful for first-time horse owners.

www.equinerescue.com
International listings of rescue
operations in Canada, Europe, and
the U.S.

www.equisearch.com
Guide to hundreds of sites,
including live chats with experts.

www.eventers.co.nz
Excellent links to equestrian
resources and events in New
Zealand.

www.haynet.net
A broad-ranging directory.

www.horsecity.com
Extensive listings; also links to an
excellent article, "Emergency Aid
on the Road," by Michael Lowder,
D.V.M.

www.horsesinamerica.com
Useful breed and rescue sites.

www.hiway16.com/horse/links.asp
Horse activities in British
Columbia.

www.horsesincanada.com
Helpful links.

www.horse-directory.co.uk
An extensive list of categories
related to equestrian topics and
concerns in the U.K.

www.horseweb.com
Many links, directories, and classi-
fied ads.

www.horsewelfare.8k.com
Lists welfare and rescue organiza-
tions by state in the U.S.

www.tashorse.com.au
Links to clubs, associations, and
horse resources in Australia.

Index